# The Best Revenge

## A Great Life

By Lauren P. Brown

# DEDICATION

This book is dedicated to
everyone who was forced
to reinvent themselves
whether or not by their choosing.

# Table of Contents

# ACKNOWLEDGMENTS

I suppose I should start off by thanking my exes for giving me something to write about – but I won't. The Best Revenge is living a great life without them.

However, I do really want to publicly thank each person who helped me through this crazy time – and who were part of me truly reaching "A Great Life."

# BACKDROP

## Behind the Scenes

- ❖ Preface

- ❖ Chart of Who's Who

- ❖ Their Connection to The Story

- ❖The Anger Element

# Preface

Never in a million years did I think I would be writing this book. I never planned to be divorced – let alone twice. One divorce, I initiated; one divorce my now-ex-husband initiated.

Initially, I was both blindsided and devasted by the second divorce – which is why my recovery story is more than noteworthy; it's worth sharing. I share this story in hopes of helping others through their divorce and into their own divorce recovery. Note: We never can or will reach 100% *recovered* – there will always be things that tug at our heart.

If you had ever told me during the devastation of the second divorce that I would be on the other side of it with wisdom to share, I would have been so hurt by you dismissing the severity of the loss that I would have slammed that friendship door shut and walked hard away from you, forever. Yet here we are.

The Background section is included solely for the purpose of your understanding - about growing up, pre-divorce times, and the divorces. Those stories are included so that you, the reader, can connect link the backstory and understand why those things that happened had such an impact.

Occasionally *[okay, often]*, a mini backstory vignette is included within other chapters, to help you, the reader, relate that chapter.

Of course, there were great times within the marriages, and I acknowledge I also have responsibility for the failed marriages. However, neither is what this book is about. Therefore, there will be very little mention of them.

Although, the book is written from the Ex-Wife perspective for obvious reasons, early readers stated that a lot of this book relates to either gender. For that reason, the pronouns used will be "they" instead of she/he.

I'm from Boston. I am sassy by nature; I can't help it – and there is sass throughout the book. For added humor, I encourage you to read the sassy sections with an attitude. You can often identify these sassy comments [*through this font style*].

I truly hope you have chosen to read this book for enjoyment purposes. But for those who want to know if <u>anyone</u> understands what you are going through, perhaps I do. I *do <u>not</u>* promote divorce; however, in a few cases, I have been known to recommend it.

Full Disclosure: Unlike many of you, I did not have to deal with child custody issues in either divorce. Due to the lack of firsthand knowledge in that area, for this non-fiction book, there are only make a few suggestions.

Watch for the Key Point at the end of the chapters starting at in the Broken section.
I have a very strong faith in God and have NO DOUBT that His intervention brought me to the point to be able to share this with you – and quite quickly. HOWEVER, this book will not be a bible study nor is there any Holier Than Thou. I do include bits and pieces of my faith when applicable and have saved the last chapter to be all about His divine intervention.

If you are being dragged through the muck and mire of divorce right now, please know I am cheering you on. Life will be different – but you are quite likely to find the "you" that you thought had long vanished.

Just remember – you have a perfect 100% score of overcoming bad days, this is just another…which may last for a season - but it too will end.

*Lauren*

**You got this!**

# Chart of Who's Who

I am opting to exclude the names of my spouses or children. This removes their identity, and the reason why may surprise you. This approach is NOT for their privacy [*frankly, I don't care about their privacy*]. It is because they are not entitled to have any recognition. Even in regular conversation, I only refer to them as the EX-ponents: X1 & X2.

My children (with X1), who are adults, are referred to as Oldest &/or Daughter and Youngest and/or Son

X2's only child daughter/my former stepdaughter, will be referred to as Singleton. Her mother is referred to as 1st Wife.

There will be a few descriptive "names" scattered throughout (i.e., Mr. Cling-on). This just helps describe the person via personality trait (i.e., Mr. Snuggles) among the common nouns/ pronouns.

## WHO'S WHO

| | |
|---|---|
| X1 | First husband; warehouse worker |
| Oldest/ Daughter | My Daughter with X1 |
| Youngest/ Son | My Son with X1 |
| X2 | Second husband; teacher; Brother #4 (youngest of 4 boys) |
| Singleton | X2's only-child daughter |
| 1st Wife | X2's wife, mother of Singleton |

## INCOGNITO in ILLINOIS

| | |
|---|---|
| Capitalcity | The state capital, about 1 ¾ hours away from Smalltown |
| Smallcity | The city where I taught school; under an hour away from Smalltown |
| Smalltown | The Midwest town I lived with both exes; they both still lived there |
| Southcity | The city I moved to when I separated from X1 |
| TheVillage | The tiny town just past Small City; 1 hour away from Smalltown and my exes |

# Chapter 1
## Living the Great Life

*Revenge (noun). The action of inflicting hurt or harm on someone for an injury or wrong suffered at their hands.*
*Ex: "Other spurned wives have taken public revenge on their husbands.[1]"*

When I looked for an "official" dictionary definition of *revenge*, I was taken aback that the example sentence was of wives getting revenge on their husbands. I feel like I might have chosen a movie scenario like a crime boss or something. To be completely honest, I was even *more surprised* by my reaction than the example sentence.

I realized I was borderline *offended* by the given example and came to the realization that I really do not want the above listed definition on either of my exes. That realization confirmed for me that I truly have moved beyond the hurt and the anger, to completing recovery.

George Herbert is cited as the first to say: "Living well is the best revenge." I have taken the liberty of tweaking it a bit to fit my life, which serves as a bit of a mantra for me: "Revenge is living my best life without him." I often use that tagline when I post pictures on Facebook showing my "best life" aka "The Great Life."

---

[1] Lexico Powered by Oxford Dictionary:
https://www.lexico.com/en/definition/revenge

**Lauren P Brown**
Jun 23 · 🌐

It's been said, and I now say it often, the best revenge is living a great life without them. Would not have believed that could be true but I'm loving life!

I assure you, getting to this point was no walk in the park.  This is evident through the frequent struggles with "what side of the grass" (a euphemism for suicide) I wanted to be on.

I did not have any desire for revenge early on; I was too hurt to even *think* about revenge… but…

As time passed… I did start thinking about revenge – quite a bit.  The lies by X1 to my adult children causing them to disown me, the attacks on my character and straight betrayal from X2, and the fact that I didn't receive a DIME from either ex (details in their chapters) was fueling my desire to get even.

Then, there was the plausibility and strong likelihood that the two exes joined forces to enhance their damage (more on this later) which made me <u>crave</u> *some* type of payback.  I wanted to hurt them for how badly they hurt me. I could easily justify retaliation; certain that "a jury of MY peers wouldn't convict me."

I had come up a list of what I thought were some really great ideas: *[Note: "Don't Try This at Home" – this is NOT a to-do list. Read the ENTIRE book, then decide… to <u>not</u> do <u>any</u> of them].*

- I could give out their cell phone numbers to the creepy people on dating sites – funny, but nah.

- I could give their personal information to the spammers who tried to get me to "date" them… blech on many levels.

- I could create dating site accounts for them – on the trashiest, raunchiest of sites.  Ewwww, no.X1 worked in a warehouse that performed random drug checks and I knew he occasionally smoked pot before it was legalized…
  hmmm – I could drop a dime every so often and have them keep "randomly" drug testing him. Ok, no.

- X2 was a teacher... I could sign him up for nasty porn sites using his school email address which he would open on his school computer *[this would be extra funny since he is Mr. Chill]* ...
  But I would never get the benefit to watch his expression... eh... but, no.

- I had copies of the joint tax returns; I had their social security numbers... I could have had many options of to impact the credit of the men who were so OBSESSED about money...
  However, that would also be <u>highly illegal</u> – therefore, that's a hard NO from me.

I have always said, "'til death do us part' does not say natural causes – I have checked" and was fairly certain that jury of my peers would not convict me... but did not want to test my theory.

I have no doubt that I would be caught; I suck as a guilty person – when questioned, I would probably giggle. Plus, I have a hard enough time remembering what exactly *did* happen; there was *no way* I could survive repeated questioning and mistruths.

Most importantly, I swore I would NEVER go to jail over one of those spousal yahoos – <u>especially</u> once we were divorced! Therefore, I just purged revenge from my consciousness.I, did however, have a couple of friends who disagreed with my position not to do *anything*, particularly to *X2*, so they appointed themselves designated revenge-getters. Neither engaged in anything harmful or illegal, they just sent photo texts to him. *As a teacher, X2 has posted his phone number in many places, so they were easily able to find it on their own.*

After only few months, my weight loss was becoming quite noticeable. As I was starting to love my body again, I posted a selfie.

A friend told me she sent this screenshot to (X2) of one of the before and after photos I had posted about my weight loss.

*Not sorry.*

Another friend sent a picture to X2 on CHRISTMAS EVE of me in a little black dress, 30 pounds lighter, that I had worn to a Christmas party… saying he was the salesman that X2 and I had met while looking for a camper.

Merry Christmas! This is Brian@***. Just sending you a pic of your ex - WOW! Didn't realize how smoking hot she is!! Thanks for the introduction. Have a (***) wild Christmas!! I will.

**That friend said the text to my ex was his Christmas gift to me.** *Not gonna lie, I thought – and still think – it was hysterical.*

Those two texts will probably ALWAYS make me smile, but for reasons you would not expect:

- ✓ The first photo was only a forwarded a screenshot of my before (the "before" picture was taken on our one-year wedding anniversary) and after my weight-loss posting.

- ✓ No harm, no foul.  There was nothing directly harmful to X2 — *well, aside from the sting of receiving that photo on Christmas Eve.*

HOWEVER, the biggest reason they will always bring a smile to my face is that I had nothing to do with the texts, confirming neither ex was taking up space in my head!

The NUMBER ONE REASON **NOT** to seek revenge on anyone is that your ex is not entitled to take up ANY real estate in your head – the doors on that property have been slammed shut and foreclosed on.

Even just contemplating revenge opens the door to your psyche, *ushering in* the person who hurt you deeply.  Each time you open that emotional door, you rehash the memories of all the ways that person hurt you. Be intentional and focused on healing the effects of those hurts and keeping that memory door shut tight

*Key Point: Revenge keeps your ex in easy-recall memory mode*

# Chapter 2
# But I'm Really Angry

As you re-live what that person did to you, the hurt fuels your anger. When you are continuously fueling the anger, you can't squash the fire to heal and move into the next season of life.

Perhaps consider the ingredients to the Anger Recipe:

## Anger is made up of: fear, hurt, and frustration.

Consider looking at each ingredient and recognize anger is the end-result of the combination of the ingredients.

Does that change your perspective?

Perhaps, when you view your hurt through the filter of the individual ingredients, you can stand up to your toughest critic - yourself [*i.e., berating yourself "How could I have been so stupid - again?"*].

# Ingredients of Anger

---

### RECIPE:  ANGER

---

*From the kitchen of*:  You and your life

*Serves*:  Likely one person directly, but leftovers can be served to anyone you encounter

*Cook Time*: Time varies depending upon the offense

*Oven Temp*: Steaming to Raging

*INGREDIENTS*

- Fear
- Hurt
- Frustration

*DIRECTIONS*

Add a heaping dose of Fear, Hurt, and Frustration to your psychological pot.  Allow to boil and fester.

When the concoction starts overflows the pot, your anger is ready to be transferred and shared in all areas of Everyday Life.

---

Consider this:  You have just gashed open your toe, hand, elbow, whatever... Ever notice how many MORE times you will unintentionally hit that <u>exact same spot?</u>

Like a repetitive injury, each time you dwell on revenge, you have ripped off the psychological first aid and ripped open the wound again.

We typically try to *prevent* pain in our lives, intentionally avoiding things that we know cause us pain *[well, except maybe the frozen margarita brain freeze...]*. Then WHY allow yourself to keep re-hurting the most sensitive part of your inner being?

Buddha is purported to have said, "Holding on to anger is like taking a poison pill and expecting the other one to die." Revenge is just taking the poison pill - again and again.

Like doing shots of that one alcohol that made you puke <u>so</u> bad many years ago that, to this day, you still can barely even look at it *[some of us clearly understand the reference]*. At the time, it seemed really, really fun – until reality hit.

The reason that, to this day, you still feel a reaction is likely due to the reality that you had too much of it. It was good in the beginning, so you kept having more and more, because the enjoyment from it quickly wore off. Then at some point, usually a bit too late, you realized you needed to stop before things got out of control. Out of nowhere came the lasting effects that had ill *[literal and figurative]* consequences.

At what point would your revenge reach the status of you being satisfied? When would it be "enough?" The answer is NEVER. Once the line has been crossed, it will never be enough. Like any addiction, do not try even a little taste - just walk away.

# Steps To Living A Great Life

These will be unpacked with more details throughout the book. Here is a general overview of what's to come:

## That's What Friends Are For
My gal pals were INSTRUMENTAL in my recovery. Everything from helping me pack, to calling me 3 times a day to be sure I wasn't thinking about the wrong side of the grass – let your friends help.

## NOT Everyone is Your Friend
In this sink or swim scenario, you don't need anyone or anything weighing you down. Anyone who is not FOR you is AGAINST you. When you feel like you're drowning, or barely treading water, cut all ties to the faux friends.

## Sometimes Divorce IS the Only Option
This will never be my favorite option, but sometimes it needs to be, and that's okay.

## Throw A Pity Party
Give yourself time to just bawl your eyes out. You deserve it. But, when the day ends, so does the party.

## Complete the Grieving Process
Although we typically associate grieving with physical death, you must consider this as the death of the relationship and life together. You will need to process this loss of relationship as though something died – because it did.

## It's a New Beginning; Rediscover Who "You" Are
You get to define this season of your life. What is it going to look like?

## Throw the Divorce Party

Even though the divorce process SUCKED, celebrate that it is <u>done</u> AND celebrate with those come-alongside the people who were instrumental in helping you through it.

## Lose THEIR Identity/Find Your Own

In general, the handful of times that I might talk about them, I refuse to use the exes' names. They are just X1 and X2 – the ugly stepbrothers of Thing 1 and Thing 2.

## Do Things and STOP Doing Things - JUST BECAUSE

"Because I can" and "Because I don't want to" are mighty powerful words.

## Know Your Triggers

There will be dates and places that trigger memories that will hurt your heart. Know what they are and avoid them. Remember, it's okay to say no (see above).

## Do Good for Others

There is something cathartic about helping someone in need. Warm your heart by helping others. "If you want to lift yourself up, lift up someone else," (Booker T. Washington).

## Get an Unconditional Lover

Go to the animal shelter and get yourself a fur baby. You will see gratitude every day of their lives, be loved in ways no human can, and change both of your lives.

## Learn to Love Yourself

This will likely be the toughest step. I felt unlovable, especially after what X2 did. I truly needed to unlearn my self-perception.

## Learn to Love Your Body

Losing weight is what helped boost my confidence – I even catch myself frequently checking out my new shape.    Love your body by becoming a healthier you.

## Make New Memories

Start your own holiday traditions; create new traditions and memories for whatever YOU choose.

## Date Again, but only if you WANT to

I used to think that I hated being alone - while simultaneously hating the idea of dating.

I have come to realize I <u>love</u> being alone.  But I also enjoy dating *[I may have become a serial dater -one after another]*.

# BACKSTORY

Set of events leading to the main story

---

- ❖ Early Days Affect Later Years

- ❖ Married in Massachusetts

- ❖ Over and Out

- ❖ Being Nice Got Me Screwed

- ❖ Too Quick on the Rebound

- ❖ Personal Foul on the Rebound

- ❖ Conspiracy Theory

# Chapter 3
# Early Days Affect the Later Years

I was born at St. Elizabeth's Hospital in Boston; grew up in Somerville, Massachusetts, which shares the town line with Boston.

If Somerville sounds vaguely familiar, it is likely because you've heard of the Winter Hill Gang and the FBI-Most Wanted mob boss, Whitey Bulger. When I was an adult with children, I found out from my dad that the WHG was not at the top of Winter Hill like I had thought *(we were at the bottom of it)*, but in the auto shop beside the alley I used to walk to school through 8th grade.

 Dad 'clarified': "Safest place in town – they didn't want the police and would never hurt kids" … parenting of the 70's. "You probably waved at Whitey," my dad said.  Knowing that I pretty much waved or said to just about anyone, there is a *very* strong likelihood I greeted the former FBI Most Wanted… on a very regular basis.  [insert face palm here].

I grew up with the inner-city experiences without the public-school education. I attended St. Ann's School, a Catholic school, from 3rd through 8th grade.  My years served there still play in my head, even as an adult.  There is a very good reason the saying "I survived Catholic School" is a statement of fact.

They didn't know about ADHD a million years ago, so they just thought I was a loud *(well, that's true)*, disruptive unfocused child – certainly must be demonic possessed.  EVERY DAY, at least once a day, some adult would tell me: "You're going to hell!"

The most in trouble I think I ever got was when I replied, "I KNOW – you tell me EVERY day!"   If I was going to hell, I was going to make it worth the trip!  I was a bit of a wild child.  In fact, at my reunion for Matignon, a Catholic high school in Cambridge, MA, one former classmate said, "That ministry cover is good… what are you *really* doing."

One not-nice-human/nun, Sister Mary Myles, was convinced that I would never finish college, IF I even completed high school.  When I started working on my PhD, X1 asked: "When will you stop trying to appease the dead nun's voices?"  "When I run out of degrees."  I have earned a few (I'm a nerd):

- Associates in Business Management
- Bachelors in Business Administration
- Bachelors in Religious Studies
- Masters in Ministry; Minor in education
- (Almost completed) Masters in Psychology
  (*didn't want to do another thesis project*)
- PhD in Human Behavior

Those voices of being stupid and not graduating are now dead and buried (this will be important later) … just like those nuns.

My interest in Psychology and Human Behavior stemmed from my mother being a victim of Bi-Polar and Schizophrenia.  She had roughly a five-year repeating pattern.

She'd take her meds faithfully, then somewhat, then not at all, then get admitted for several months to a behavioral health center (formerly referred to as a 'mental hospital'), get on track with her medication, get discharged, and begin the cycle again.

I had a great number of "other mothers" – family friends who stepped in to fill the maternal duties (i.e., Mrs. Sugrue made African Stew for our International Day – twice, because I dropped the first one getting out of the car.)

Due to the number of times my mother was hospitalized and her changes in behavior throughout the cycle, we had a deplorable relationship.

I found out six months before she passed, when my children were in THEIR TWENTIES, that my mother held a grudge against me for being a rebellious teenager. The grudge was finally dissolved after I told her that rebellion is a stage that all teenagers go through. What a waste for the Mother/Daughter relationship.

My biggest fear in life was that I would end up with the same type of relationship with my daughter (this is also important for later).

# Chapter 4
# Married In Massachusetts

I met X1 at a Halloween party that I didn't want to go to, in part because it was "out in the boondocks" – Littleton, MA. "Anything west of Lexington, might as well be California." But I went anyway.

X1 was Dracula; I was a nun *[based on my first-hand knowledge how scary they could be]*. We met because I continuously hid <u>behind</u> him many times that night because the Hostess' brother was Mr. Touchy-Feely... and I was trying to avoid him. By the end of the night, we exchanged numbers.

When I finally saw Drac without his green-faced Dracula makeup, I thought he was smoking hot. After we were together about 6 months, we moved in together.

That went along for about 2 years before he proposed. I should have seen the red flags then:
- He would talk to me about getting married and yet he would tell his best friend (who was dating my best friend) something TOTALLY different
  - *(sarcasm font)* Of course, he was so charming, he must be telling the truth
- He used to make me feel that I was in a race against time, but he was *okay* with settling down with me...
  (I was 24 years old).
- Four different times I started packing my stuff to leave
- He was an EXCEPTIONALLY different person when we were around other people *(Narcissism 101)*.

We got married, moved to a Boston suburb, had two kids. The suburb was less than an hour outside of Boston, one town away from a Simon Properties mall with a 15 theater megaplex. We were about 20 minutes to more 'rural' areas for corn mazes, animal zoos, and 'haunted' farms.

At that time, we also both began our relationship with God (*I had left the Catholic faith*). Church and Sunday School seemed to help shape him into a good husband and a great dad.

In 2007, we made the decision to leave Massachusetts, accepting my Children's Ministry position in Smalltown, Midwest, a great place for the kids to grow up. One key factor in deciding to move was that the cost of living in Massachusetts was (still is) astronomical; Midwest living is a mere fraction of the cost.

Smalltown is a quiet town which seems trapped in the 70's – in the summer, it was a BIG DEAL that the first Friday of every month to go to the Park n' Cruise – people parking their antique cars and other people walking around and looking at them… the SAME cars that are there each month. We would walk down with the dogs for popcorn & snacks just for something to do.

Smalltown is home to a small D1 university. While you would think there would be lots of activities for college kids; you'd be wrong. Smalltown is the POLAR OPPOSITE of the Massachusetts suburban town with NOTHING to do locally and 2-3 <u>hours</u> to any major attraction,

# Chapter 5

# Over and Out

As the kids grew up, X1 and I grew apart. While some of it was gradual, there were some events that added credence that my decision was based on more than we "just grew apart."

## Big Issue #1 Mocking Ministry

Imagine leaving everyone and everything you know to move 1200 miles away for your wife's ministry job – only to have her LOSE that job two years later due to church politics – disagreeing with the pastor over the "need" for a $1 million building addition in a dying college town (this will be important later).

While my daughter and I clung tighter to God, both X1 and my son walked HARD away from God. The Youngest said, "We moved here for God and God SCREWED us."

Hindsight made me realize that this was the beginning of the long, difficult road to the end.

X1 perceived EVERYTHING through its worst-case scenario *(I could fill a BOOK on that alone – nope, don't care)*. I, on the other hand, am an obnoxious optimist, finding something good in even horrible situations (i.e., the day of the 9/11 attacks on America, I pointed out that Congress had united together on the steps to pray for our country).

Walking away from his faith transformed X1 into an angry, bitter pessimist. The hope once found in Jesus was replaced by sheer negativity.

I had earned a master's degree in Ministry, therefore I continued working in ministry, pouring salt on his faith-wound. Losing his faith was sucking the life out of me - then he started mocking MY faith.

At first, X1 used passive aggression to attack my faith. For a while, he and the kids were still attending church. X1 would drive BELOW the speed limit on the way to church *[the man who didn't believe in 'slow' who got pulled over going 85 MPH coming off a highway ramp in Ohio with his wife and kids in the car]*.

Doing so, he *knew* stressed me out *[you know... arriving late to service late so everyone turns around and stares]*. After a while, X1 just stopped attending – which was fine with me, I could keep my focus where it needed to be.

For Christmas one year, I asked for my family to join me at Christmas Eve service. After a lot of cajoling, X1 and Youngest agreed to join me; those two then proceeded to ridicule and mock everything about the Christmas Eve service and laugh throughout the whole thing.

I was not only embarrassed but infuriated. It was not a very merry Christmas that year.

## Big Issue #2 Thinks I'm Dumb

 X1 has a serious inferiority complex regarding education because he never completed his associate degree. His means to compensate, therefore, would be to make me feel stupid *(remember Sister Mary Myles).*

X1 constantly tried to appear educated, *(see Are They a Narcissist chapter)* often giving opinions or made-up data as statements of fact. I had no problem pointing out he was wrong. The Knowledge War happened daily, sometimes multiple times a day.

## Big Issue #3 Car Troubles

In December 2016, while traveling highway speed (70+), a full-sized buck (deer) jumped out in front of my minivan. I hit the deer, the deer TOTALLED my car – and that bleeping-bleep deer didn't die!!! He ran off into the woods *[enter not-nice-words here]!* When I called X1 to tell him what had happened, he never even asked if I was okay. He was NOT happy.

X1 told me several times about how I inconvenienced him *[from watching TV],* when he came and pick me up from the side of the highway.    He also was not happy needing to share a vehicle until I could get a replacement minivan to schlep 2 high school-aged kids, their friends, and all their stuff.

I did all the insurance paperwork; I was able to find another minivan in the amount of the insurance check.  I didn't like the replacement van anywhere near as much as the van the deer destroyed… in fact, I really didn't like it much at all – but it would serve its purpose.

Three months later, on Palm Sunday, that van and I had a roll-over accident on icy roads, down into a ditch *[first I spun, then I rolled, then I came to a full and sudden stop]*. When I did stop, I called my husband.

When the paramedics arrived, one asked, "Who is screaming at you on that phone?" "My husband." "Hang that up." So, I did.

X1 called back — now infuriated that I hung up on him AND totaled a second car in three months — even though one was caused by a deer and the other by ice.

In the Emergency Room, X1 had to be <u>escorted</u> OUT because he was screaming AGAIN about it. That was about the time my son arrived - because X1 only called my daughter *[Daddy's Girl]*, not my son. The Youngest heard his mother was in a roll-over accident from the Oldest, when she was wondering why he was not yet at the hospital.

Both accidents triggered their own injuries and recovery processes — but since I "caused" those accidents (again, the deer ran in front of me and an ICE STORM), he had ZERO interest in providing care during my recovery.

X1 had always struggled with providing care/caring for me anyway. He would be great the first day or two; by Day 3, he would run out of patience because he felt I should have been recovered by then *[ya know, Pneumonia, C-section, or other surgeries...]*. This reduced level of patience for care was then exacerbated anytime a financial impact was attached to it.

### Enough is Enough

In Sept 2016, I began the process of filing for divorce. I reminded X1 of all the times I had threatened to leave and that I was now starting the process. I was done and he knew it.

Unfortunately, there was no way I would be able to afford the house payments, etc., on my own – we were barely financially stable with two incomes; there was no way I could survive on one income. I paused the process.

In December 2016, I accepted a job an hour away from the house. I told him I would be moving there as a trial separation. He needed to decide what he wanted to do; I would not be back unless he changed how he treated me [*this chapter could drag on and on and on about everything he pulled – Ain't nobody got time for 'dat*].

## Big Issue #4 Final Straw Happy Birthday- NOT!

February 8th, I called X1 and asked if he wanted to come to Southcity *(where I now was living)* for dinner the following night. In the most condescending tone, he said, "What would I want to do THAT for?"

Disgusted, I replied, "So your WIFE doesn't celebrate her 50th birthday alone."

"Yeah, if I've got nothing else to do." Well, he came to Southcity, we went to some cheap place for dinner, then ended at Home Depot, buying a sink for our house in Smalltown. I got bath towels, for my birthday gift [*Happy 50th – yay me*].

My birthday present to myself: move forward with the divorce.

# Chapter 6
# Being Nice Got Me Screwed

## The Settlement

This certainly could evolve into its own chapter, but I do not want to give that much literary real estate to it. I am including the overview to show I know what it's like to lose hard in divorce.

I just wanted to be DONE. I was tired of getting sucked down his Black Hole of Pessimism.

I was entitled to SO much money: Monthly maintenance (alimony), part of his retirement plan, sale of the house if he sold it or cash out from the equity when he refinanced. *[How horrible must a person be for the one entitled to the money not take ANY of it?]*

I KNEW X1 could not afford to keep the house and pay alimony. I had hoped we could have civil dinners together or something; I didn't want the house to *have* to be sold.

I waived ALL but the equity in attempts to maintain civility so that it would not affect my relationship with the children (remember the relationship with my mother and my biggest fear). It wasn't about the money; I just wanted to be DONE.

I made it VERY CLEAR to X1 that the reason I was doing so was to maintain peace in the family and not disrupt my relationship with the now-adult children (this will also be important later).

When I pushed back with my rights, he reminded me that he had a gun in the house. Suddenly, I was afraid for my life (this will be important later).

X1 packed what HE selected that I could have, I picked it up from the garage – all the while, terrified he would shoot me. He couldn't be bothered giving back things like my dance recital costumes, a stuffed dog I got when I was 3 years and in the hospital at Christmas, my record albums, or pick from JOINT PROPERTY, etc. *[Great guy, huh?]*

I tried to make our divorce civil. I tried to be nice – until he told me I could not enter OUR house to get my items and choose from the joint property even though, legally, I had every right to do so.

It was at that very moment that I suddenly became terrified of the man I had been married to for 25 years. ANY time I saw him, it freaked me out and I left abruptly (this will be an important detail later).

I was quite happy to just not have him in my life anymore… or so I thought.

# Chapter 7

# Too Quick on the Rebound

I swore I would NEVER marry again; I barely wanted to date again. While separated from X1, I dated a few guy friends who were happy that I was separated, in the process of becoming single. Eh... but it was just too weird moving from friend-zone to romance.

May 2017, while walking into a graduation party, X2 was walking out. We chatted for a really long time by the entrance. We had been friends for a while and then fell out of touch. He taught at the high school my kids were at; he was The Youngest's favorite teacher.

I had been a licensed English teacher in Massachusetts (Rural Midwest only recently took my license to return to teaching) so X2 and I would chat about nerdy teacher type of stuff.

X2 also had proofread my master's thesis for me.

We always had a cool connection, but he was married, I was married; I had no idea we could ever be anything more than friends.

As we were talking, he told me that he was divorced last month; I told him I would be divorced by the end of summer. We both talked about how our lives changed, living alone, and so on.

I mentioned that I was finishing up my dissertation, etc. He offered to again do major proofreading for me. We got together roughly once a week to eat dinner with someone and go over the suggested corrections.

By the end of June, we were starting to think this would move forward romantically; the first date would be the Red, White, and Boom – (RiverCity's July 4th celebration). We'd joked about how there were two different types of fireworks that night.

He was just sooo sweet. He would send AMAZING good morning texts, telling me how much he loved me; bring flowers for no reason... and of course, the intimacy was beyond words. We used to comment and agree that we had a very high level of intimacy, and that sex was just a small part of it.

I reminded him <u>often</u> to be his real self, to not become a different person (this will be important later) if we got married.

Shortly thereafter, my lease would be running out. Since we were nearly always together. Why pay 2 rents, 2 utilities, etc.?

Our relationship went from friends to cohabitating IN FOUR MONTHS!

> *On this week's edition of What NOT To Do:*
> *Moving through the steps of the relationship at sonic speed.*

It was decided that I would move back to Smalltown *("The Smalltown Vortex is real")* because he was a teacher there and I could just get a job in the town... which just so happened to be where X1 also lived.

> *In the next edition of What NOT To Do:*
> *Moving back to the town where your previous ex-husband still lives... and has a gun.*

Between X2 and I, we knew a LOT of people around town. It did not take long for the Gossip Mill to announce to the entire town we were dating.

There was one VERY LARGE problem with this: X1 told my children that X2 and I had been having an affair. Not only that, but that we had been having an affair for TEN YEARS *[interesting math: moved to Smalltown in 2007, I graduated in 2009 with the thesis he proofread; divorced from X1 in 2017 – we had only been IN Smalltown for 10 years]*.

In hindsight, and through various research in my human behavior program, I NOW recognize that we were both victims of Love Trauma Syndrome, unresolved emotional scars from a broken heart. Neither of us was in a healthy position to start dating… let alone ZOOM through the steps of relationship building, and cannonball into marriage.

At first, I didn't worry about such a ridiculous accusation because I was certain my now-adult children would remember that during the time I was allegedly having that affair, there is no possible way I could have squeezed it in among: my FOUR part-time jobs, my PhD coursework, being at EVERY sporting and school event, AND making sure to have a family dinner ready every night – sometimes for as many as 10 people, because the kids' friends would often stay for dinner.

I didn't think much about the ridiculous accusation because I was certain that my intelligent adult children would remember that when we supposedly were having an affair, X2 had cancer. I didn't even KNOW he <u>had</u> cancer… I certainly didn't drive the 1.5+ hours to see him while he was in the hospital, or even help him get settled in when he got home.

Surely, they would recognize that I never made the man one meal while he was recovering <u>by himself</u> (I ALWAYS made meals for friends sick or recovering from surgery).

These two adult children had witnessed decades of their father's on-going verbal assaults and his self-centeredness that reared its ugly head often. I sacrificed what I wanted to do for what the kids wanted or needed. My children who both graduated college in 4 years, with honors. Surely, they would be smart enough to know the truth, right?

WRONG. They 100% believed their father's lie.

Because of the lies from X1 about X2, **my daughter committed the cruelest act a daughter could do to her mother**: not only was I not to have any role in her wedding, but moreover was told I was not welcome to attend — to the extent that the location would not even be disclosed to me.

Not trying to get "high score" on anyone's Level of Hurt chart but being banned from her daughter's wedding will always rank in the list of Top Five Worst Divorce Outcomes.

I actually HAD a terrible relationship with my mother — with plenty of tangible reasons to exclude her, and I still did not do something so cruel to her.

I waived nearly every PENNY from the divorce to keep peace with the kids — and X1 took that too. He KNEW that would absolutely devastate me; he was right (remember my biggest fear).

Through all of those gut-wrenching hurts, X2 was amazing; he would always say "I'll love you through it." When we were dating, knowing how much I HATED Mother's Day *(by this point, my mother has passed and my children won't even acknowledge that I birthed them)*, he would make plans for a fun filled day to take my mind off it. However, like many other things that changed once we were married – X2 believed he no longer needed to "love me though that hurtful holiday." He didn't think he needed to be the same person that I dated (remember I told him to be real in the beginning...). Whatever.

He was Mr. Chill; I tried to be Mrs. Chill. I was SOOO in love with this man, I loved him so hard I lost myself in him.

X2 would tell me how much it hurt his feelings whenever we argued. Therefore, I would try really, really hard to give in to what he wanted to avoid hurting his feelings. The problem with this approach, however, is that disagreements never got resolved. His feelings got hurt; the "discussion" ended.

There's a wee bit of a problem when a strong, independent, Irish woman from Boston stuffs her emotions for too long....
I would just 'go Boston.' The eruption of all those stuffed emotions would parallel that eruption of Mt. St. Helen's. It meant that EVEEERRRYTHING that had been stuffed since the previous eruption was busting its way up and out... destructive to everything in its path.

Even though I tried SO hard to not argue because it "hurt his feelings;" the narcissist viewed my arguments as defiance anyway– something that the perpetrator *(me)* would experience dire consequences for later.

Then COVID hit. We were quarantined together AND teaching from home.  We shared each other's misery with remote teaching, making sure we had downtime together to recharge and regroup.  As far as I knew, we were handling quarantining quite well *[nope]*.

COVID took a lot of important social markers away from students.  As a teacher of Senior English, he knew those students well, some since Freshman year.  He was excited for Prom, for Graduation, for After Prom – all the fun times together before they are no longer together… and they never happened.

One day in early May, an exchange student down the street was getting ready to leave.  Students did a drive by, beeping and waving, ensuring social distancing.  X2 stood on the porch with tears in his eyes.  THAT, I firmly believe, was the beginning of the depression spiral. From there, he just lost his joy, his vitality, who he really was.

In July, we went camping in Michigan *[as usual – where he was from]*.  Three of the four brothers had made plans for a camping trip, with the ladies coming along.  I liked hanging out with the ladies; those gals were awesome… but the brothers together… *[enter not nice words here]*.  Interestingly enough, X2 used to tell me how 1st Wife refused to go to any of his family events with him. *[Hmmm…. If only there may have been a good reason…]*

X2 *(Brother #4)* idolized Brother #2, the 2nd oldest brother, who always protected X2, his baby brother. While I liked that brother and loved his long-term girlfriend, X2's personality would completely change around him, particularly how he treated me around him.

In hindsight, knowing that Brother 2's first wife staged her own "Missing Person" disappearance, without a trace - including leaving her kids behind, only to find out a few months later that she had begun a new life an hour way – probably should have been a larger warning flag than it was.

When Brothers 2, 3, and 4 were together, Brothers 2 and 4 were just VILE to Brother 3; Brother 3 is VERY different from the other two.

Ironically, I related better to Brother #3 at these Brother gatherings. Brother #3 had been married to the same woman for decades, serving more as a caregiver for her, due to several falls from horses without a helmet. Brother 3 was the only brother of the 4 boys to never have divorced.

The brothers behaved so deplorably at the campground one night, the following day I went and apologized to our elderly camping neighbors who certainly heard the whole thing.

At the end of the week, we went to X2's best friend's daughter's COVID delayed graduation party, where more of his rude behaviors came out. After a week of tension, X2's behavior at the party was my final straw.

He had treated me horribly in front of his family & friends all week; by the time we got back to our camper, I was seething. Never a good thing for people with strong personalities to stuff hurts and frustrations… and by the end of a week of this foolishness, I had had **enough**! I. Was. **MAD.**

I walked around the campground, trying to calm down — but it didn't help. All I could think of was "Oh my gosh, 'Until death do us part' is going to require a lot of counseling."

The eruption of stuffed emotions may have been similar to that of Pompei: vicious and fatal. I admit I was mighty nasty during that argument. Therefore, in true narcissistic fashion, the retribution had to a destructive, hurtful, shallow means of destruction.

# Chapter 8
# Personal Foul on the Rebound

You know how rebound dating is bad; rebound marriage is worse. This was a very hard chapter to begin to write; it meant I needed to revisit some horrible hurts. Frankly, I am choosing not to provide the entire drama series – we'll save that for the made- for-TV movie. I am choosing to include some those hurts in hopes to give others the strength to press on.

The man whose calls, for three years, were answered with "Love of My Life" told me, through his lawyer, not to communicate with him ever again. I had absolutely no idea what things he had brewing. August 28, 2020 was the last time we spoke actual words to each other.

Imagine making plans in the summer with your spouse for a New Year's Eve away to someplace warm or trying three times to purchase a camper together with the plan of him retiring in 2022 so we could camp our way across the country *[hmmm: is that why he put the house on the market so early?* Whatever]. Then suddenly cannot even speak to him.

Imagine hearing he has been planning his exit for over a YEAR! Therefore, as I look back on things, it is obvious he is a liar - either he lied throughout all the sweet, loving things he said or he lied about how long he had been planning his exit.

Reality is the man that I adored for his character was nuttin' but a lying, little narcissist.

Flashback:   With a sense of urgency, I pushed for X2 to get medical help, recognizing the depression overpowering him.

I encouraged X2 to go to his primary care physician to get medication, especially as there was a waitlist for counselors. Unfortunately, the prescribed medication caused some odd side-effects (I don't remember exactly what they were now); I encouraged him to call his doctor to change the meds. He absolutely would <u>not</u> do so – I think he viewed it as disrespectful or ungrateful to his doctor.

> Side note: This doctor told him that he should go get a colonoscopy due to his age and that his insurance would cover it. Thankfully, he listened because he was found with almost to Stage 4 colon cancer.  Because she suggested getting the procedure, he placed her at a near-god status, blindly following anything she said/did – would not ever push back when there were side effects or not an exact resolution.

> I changed doctors/practices due to some inappropriate practices in her office *(instead of using medical history to prescribe which medication worked, they would give a weaker version so I would have to go back, pay another co-pay, and then get the one I should have had in the first place)*. Blue Cross/Blue Shield dropped them as approved providers.

Instead, X2 would just keep dealing with the side effects.  The one side effect had me panicked, slight suicidal ideations. Nothing specific, but rapidly becoming concerning.  I knew I couldn't go to his doctor; I thought I could tell his counselor.

I believe the whole ordeal exploded due to mental health meds. If I was to ever seek revenge on anyone, it would be this poor excuse of a marriage counselor*. I will always believe it was her manipulation that triggered this whole thing.

> Remember the church politics that caused my guys to walk away from God: *In 2009, due to some crazy church politics at the church we moved from Massachusetts for & my guys leaving their faith, there were some at the church who villainized me for not supporting a $1 million building addition project that the church could not afford. This counselor was one in that group. I believe she viewed used this situation as her God-given opportunity for restitution and for me endure the wrath.*

I had agreed to go to the 3rd counseling session with X2. I was more than willing to go because I could speak on the side effects I was seeing. However, just after we got settled in her office, she suddenly STOOD UP and started SCREAMING at me – telling me most marriages don't come back from this and that the "CHRISTIAN" COUNSELOR recommended he end our marriage. WHHHHAAAATTT?

The counselor tells me that X2 told her – *or they conjured up together* – that I had scared him *[Heck yeah, I did! Remember that camping blowup argument earlier in the book...]* and he was "afraid for his life" *[what??? Because I yelled at him?]*. She stated that the situation *[I started using the on-going unpersonal term "The Situation"]* was so serious she recommended DIVORCE without ANY marriage counseling... and recommended for X2 to attend counseling with HER for a YEAR.

However, as mentioned in the start of the book regarding revenge, I really just don't care. I did not want to constantly get status updates, provide more information, or even to have to think about it. There was no gain to pushing back on her and/or having her lose her license – plus if he WANTS to feed that cash cow for a year+ … not my problem.

I most definitely could have gained my revenge on her by reporting the highly inappropriate manipulation practices. Don't think I didn't think about it or start investigating how many places I could file complaints…But for what? He certainly did not want to reconcile.

X2 told the counselor SO many things out of context, i.e., *[read in a tattle-telling voice]*, "Moooommm, she makes me use GPS even though I know where I am going" – yeah, because GPS knew that the route we needed to take was CLOSED due to construction.

"Moooommm, she won't let me play *my* music when we are traveling." That was because he would ONLY play his music and I wanted to hear something I liked for a change. Whatever.

While in the room with the counselor, X2 said something that clicked. Suddenly, I was pretty certain that EVERYTHING he had told me about his <u>first</u> divorce WAS A LIE.

X2 had always told me that he was in the hospital in Capitalcity (about 1 ¾ hours away from home) for a week, and that 1st Wife would neither come see him nor bring Singleton to visit, saying that he didn't have any visitors all week. X2 lamented he needed to call a friend to come give him a ride home because 1st Wife would not come get him.

> Side Note: Remember the accusation that I was having an affair with him for a decade… pretty certain he would not have needed to call for a ride, and certainly not be alone after surgery.

X2 told everyone that shortly after arriving home, 1st Wife told him that she wanted a divorce. However, his daughter, Singleton, would contradict that statement, saying her mother told her that X2 divorced her mother.

X2 LOVED the pity party. A card-carrying member of the Pity Party, standing on the platform of an abandoned cancer victim *[oh what a horrible person his ex-wife is; oh, poor him]*.

When the spotlight faded, because there wasn't anything to need pity for, he created one… through me.

The man that I couldn't even disagree with because it hurt his feelings told EVERYONE that he was a victim of domestic violence, and I was "a horrible person".

hmmm… I think I see a pattern.

Then X2 blurted a phrase that confirmed my suspicion that Singleton's version was the true story. "I survived cancer; I will not be unhappy in a marriage."

IT ALL FIT. He divorces his wives, when he gets "unhappy" … *[oh, please call the Whaaa-mbulance]*.

Friday, August 28, 2020: As I was heading out the door to go to my teacher in-service before the start of the school year, he told me he would be staying at a friend's house for the weekend.

Saturday, August 29, 2020: Mr. No-Spine TEXTED me that he would not be coming back to the house until I was gone, he was filing for divorce, and I had to move out. *[His wittle feelings were hurt cuz I told him to 'man up' on more than one occasion…texting that he wanted a divorce, proves he still hadn't done so.]*

This was three DAYS before what would have been our 2nd anniversary. The betrayal and devastation were beyond words.

The worst part of this entire saga is it was likely PREMEDIATED from the START. We had signed a prenuptial agreement so that "our debt remained separated." I was so in love and CONVINCED he was such a man of integrity; I did not read it carefully.

The prenuptial included the home purchased when we were engaged be ONLY in HIS name and set me up to be penniless when he divorced me.

I came to realize that I was nothing but the tool for him to waive **$100,000 of his debt** in bankruptcy. X2 used me to drop his debt-to-income ratio, as did purchasing the house in only his name.

# Chapter 9
# Conspiracy Theory

When X2 first called the bankruptcy attorney, in June 2019, I originally had not planned to file because my debt was fairly small and quite manageable.

Unknowingly, this would create a VERY large problem for X2 who was trying to dispose of all of his **$100,000** incurred debt. X2 needed me to file to drop his debt-to-income ratio to be able to file Chapter 7; otherwise, he would have to work out repayment with his creditors.

X1 owed me $10,000 for the equity in the house, as I was signing the house over to him (reminder: he got the house, the dogs, alimony waived, kept his full pension, AND turned the kids against me).

X1 failed to make the agreed upon scheduled payments for the short sale of the house in Massachusetts and therefore the bank served me with notice of garnishment of MY wages.

 I was forced into filing bankruptcy at the insistence of X2.However, that is not even what clued me in to the conspiracy theory *(X1 knew X2 from various school events, since X2 was Youngest's favorite teacher)*. FOUR different times X1 was in front of my/X2's house at the EXACT TIME I was returned from work I was a teacher; teachers NEVER leave school at the same time every day. Plus, I might stop at the grocery store; I may be delayed by a train crossing.

There was only ONE PERSON who knew my absolute, exact time I would be home:  X2 (remember I was afraid for my life that X1 would shoot me). Was it ironic or coincidence that X2 used my words about X1: "afraid for my life" in his claim against me?

The premeditation, the drama, I felt like I was living in a Made-For-TV movie *[hmmm]*.

After the dust settled from that volcanic eruption called "my life", I then had time to look things over and analyze them – *[when you have a PhD, you analyze EVERYTHING]*.

Ironic Fact:
- Aug 28, 2017    Done Date with X1 (divorce final)
- Aug 28, 2020    Last conversation with X2


I made a simple timeline which gives credence to the intentionality and conspiracy theories.    Will I ever get anything from that discovery? Nope. *[Perhaps one day they will say they had a book written about lol.  LOL]*

# Timeline of Premeditation

| | |
|---|---|
| July 2017 | • Started dating |
| Oct 2017 | • Co-Habituated<br>• Met with Bankruptcy Atty told not enough debt to income ratio |
| Jan 2018 | • Purchased engagement ring |
| Feb 2018 | • Purchased home<br>   ○ Put only in his name |
| Aug 2018 | • VERY carefully worded prenup |
| Sept 2018 | • Married<br>• X2 bought a new truck, used my paid-off van as trade-in |
| Oct 2018 | • Lauren agrees to waive the $10k equity X1 owes<br>in exchange for him taking on the rest of the jointly owned mortgage balance |
| June 2019<br><br>*Start of theorized conspiracy* | • Lauren served order for garnishment of wages in Avidia debt<br>• Lauren is forced into filing bankruptcy |
| July 2019<br>• *Been planning about a year?"* | • Met with bankruptcy atty<br>   ○ moving forward |
| Nov 2019 | • Bankruptcy filed |

| | |
|---|---|
| Jan 2020 | <ul><li>Bankruptcy discharged</li><li>Lauren & X2 purchased car for Lauren to commute</li><li>VERY HIGH interest rate due to bankruptcy</li></ul> |
| March 2020 | <ul><li>X2 bought a new truck</li></ul> |
| May, June, July 2020 | <ul><li>X2 tried to purchase a jointly owned new camper</li></ul> |
| July 2020 | <ul><li>Combined bank accounts to one joint account</li><li>Met with atty regarding wills<ul><li>Atty did not want Lauren associated with the house</li></ul></li></ul> |
| Aug 2020 | <ul><li>X2 filed for divorce with ZERO attempts at reconciliation</li><li>Made Lauren move out of the house</li><li>Closed bank account without any notice</li></ul> |
| Oct 2020 | <ul><li>X2 moved out of the house HE owns, started paying rent</li><li>Put house on the market for $62,900 – *his purchase price even with many modern upgrades*</li><li>X2 bought a new truck</li></ul> |
| Feb 2021 | <ul><li>**Divorce FINAL!!!**</li></ul> |
| Nov 2021 | *At the time of this writing, house on the market 397 days*<br>Price dropped to $57,500 |

I tell the backstory so that you, the reader, understand that I have a bit of credibility on going divorce hell too.

I share those experiences to be able to share (I hope) helpful hints on how to get through it.

I provided just the peripheral information – or this book would be HUGE.

Okay, enough with my Should-Be-Made-For-TV-Drama.

Let's talk about you

# BROKEN

Fractured or damaged,
no longer in working order

## Life Has Changed

❖ Are They a Narcissist?

❖ Thinking It Through

❖ Throw the Pity Party

❖ Process The Grief

❖ Admit Your Part

# Chapter 10
# Are They a Narcissist?

I had no idea that I was so skilled at attracting narcissists, but I'm obviously very good at it – I <u>married</u> TWO of them. I thought I would surely recognize the signs and symptoms the second time - but I did not; primarily due to X2 hiding his real character until after we were married *(remember I told him to be his real self when we were dating).* It would infuriate him when I would say, "Must be married," because he had become <u>such</u> a different person nearly immediately after the wedding.

The first step in recovering from a narcissistic relationship is to understand that it was never about you anyway. Then you can move on to realize that the person you thought loved you more than anyone else and that would love you until the end of time… only loved you based on fulfilling their needs.

When you stop meeting their needs (X1) OR when you challenge their decision/position (X2), your spouse's narcissism shows up like the neon lights on the strip mall in Vegas! "Til death do us part" seems to be the trigger for narcissists to show their true selves – they know they have a captive/ captured participant. At that point, it will confirm this was never really about you in the first place – all about them.

This is just a simple checklist with easy examples of how both my exes presented their symptoms to aid in your understanding.

---

*Key Point: Know who and what you are dealing with*

---

| What Narcissism Looks Like | |
| --- | --- |
| Better than everyone else; entitlement<br><br>*This is what most people identify with narcissism.* | X1 loved to portray himself as the smartest person on earth.<br><br>Like a spoiled child, and citing because he survived cancer, X2 felt entitled to whatever he wanted – ALWAYS. |
| Excessive Need for Attention | X1 tried to be part of our son's friend group – trying to be center stage (with teenagers)<br><br>X2 would use his theatrical training to deliver his message. Served in coaching roles, would be offended when anyone offered suggestions |
| Lack of Empathy | UGGH the largest character flaw in both.<br><br>X1 didn't seem to understand feelings<br><br>X2's feelings were the only feelings that mattered |
| Sense of self is fragile | Both became super defensive if anyone pushed back on their sense of self. |

If you can relate to any of these points, there are great articles on-line about how to handle a narcissist.

| | |
|---|---|
| Relationships are only for what is beneficial to them | X1 I had the better paying job and education. He told me he would "become a couch potato" once I finished my PhD

X2 after only our 3rd date, X2 injected Singleton, his teenage daughter, into our relationship, frequently pushing me to take the mother role (1st Wife, her mother is still alive). Our first Christmas, he gave me an artist drawing of the three of us… we were still just dating. |
| Difficulty with attachment and dependency | X1 lacked the ability to be emotionally intimate

X2 could not be partners – he was in charge of everything |
| Frequently demeans, intimidates, bullies, or belittles others | X1 became a HUGE bully to me and categories of people (i.e., better educated)

*X2 is my height, 5'7" and the shortest of the 4 brothers. I think there was a lot of Little Man Ego going on too

X2 consistently belittled Brother #3 |

# Chapter 11
# Thinking It Through

Divorce is ugly, and painful, and a just horrible experience all around; I will never be a fan of divorce. With that said, sometimes there is just no other option.

If you are a victim of abuse, divorce IS NOT open for discussion, it is not optional. Period. Granted, that may require additional supports to facilitate leaving, etc., but staying is not in question. Note: Abuse is not limited to physical abuse; mental abuse is still abuse *[\*\*cough, cough\* X1]*. Keep in mind that both women and men can be victims of abuse *[X2 claimed he was a victim of domestic violence because I yelled at him; remember I couldn't even stand to hurt his feelings, let alone his body]*.

The Bible says the only permitted reason for divorce is adultery *[a bit odd since polygamy does appear in the Bible]*. I do know of several couples that did work through the cheating and rekindle their marriage. While it is possible to reconcile, a strong unanimous decision AND commitment is required by <u>both</u> parties to work through it.

I am not going to share the LONG process of how I made to the decision to divorce X1 *[though my lawyer did say, "I can't believe you stayed with him that long!"]*.

X2 made the "decision" for me. X2 up and decided with no notice or any attempt at counseling – there was no other *option.*

# Questions To Consider

## Before Choosing to Divorce

Here are some of my deciding/determining factors. It's not an all-inclusive checklist; apply to your situation. As you go through the list, be attentive to other questions they raise.

- ☐ Is someone in danger of being hurt or killed?
  - ○ MOVE OUT IMMEDIATELY: There is potential for further abuse by threatening divorce.
    - ▪ *I helped a friend leave her abusive husband – had a team of people ready to pack her stuff and get her out as soon as he left for work.*
  - ○ GO DIRECTLY TO DIVORCE. This is not optional. Line up your exit strategy, enlist the help of others. Do not delay! *"Do not pass Go, do not collect $200"*

- ☐ Is the situation one that needs a permanent change?
  - ○ Is this a thought-through decision?
  - ○ Is this an impulse decision *[ex: polar opposite to running off to Vegas to get married]*?
  - ○ Is it based on <u>one</u> situation of hurt feelings?
  - ○ Are your trying to get revenge?
  - ○ Is the issue(s) worth ending this relationship?

- ☐ Can you financially support yourself?

- ☐ Are children involved? How will this affect them?

- ☐ Who can be available to assist – and how can they help?

- ☐ What else should be considered?

Most importantly, you must remember that this will be a permanent solution that <u>creates</u> MORE problems. Is this really the choice you want to make? In both cases, divorce was my only option, while only one was my choice.

I am a list maker – I make lists OF lists... List absolutely EVERY reason you can think of for this decision.

Consider using a SWOT Analysis model to evaluate the good and bad points of the decision. The SWOT Analysis is a bit more focused than a pros/cons list, looking at immediate and future concerns.

Write/type these out and keep them in a place that you can review them when [not "if"] you are questioning if you made the right decision.

*Key Point: Count the costs before choosing divorce*

# Create a SWOT Analysis
## for BOTH Staying and Leaving

STRENGTHS: What are the <u>immediate advantages</u> to this decision?

WEAKNESSES:  what are the <u>immediate disadvantages</u> to your decision?

OPPORTUNITIES: What <u>future advantages and opportunities</u> this decision could present?

THREATS:  What are the <u>future disadvantages</u> to this decision?

## Questions to Consider:
- Do I really love them and want to grow old with them?
  - Confirm this is a healthy and safe decision
  - If yes, THEN STOP RIGHT HERE
    this is your answer
- Financial stability – do you have the means to financially survive on your own?
  - If not, what would need to happen to do so

- What/how many other changes would need to occur?

# HANG ON!

## IT'S GONNA BE

## A

## WILD RIDE

# Chapter 12

# **Throw the Pity Party**

Now that the divorce is in the works, you need to know there are times during this process that you will be convinced that life just sucks; that nothing good will come of it, and you have the worst life ever. Sometimes, even those of us who have followed Jesus for a long time, feel like our hope is gone.

This is a very natural response to divorce, especially during the process of being divorced. You will need to go through the emotional steps of grieving (Chapter 13).

First step, throw yourself a party. Plan this party just like you'd plan any other party:

➢ **GUEST LIST** You are inviting a VIP – YOU. You are the VIP (Very Important Person) <u>and</u> the Guest of Honor! If you want, Me, Myself, and I could also attend. That puts your party at capacity; no room for anyone else.

➢ **DATE** Choose the date and time carefully. You can throw an impromptu party whenever necessary *(I occasionally still throw one –usually following a <u>really</u> bad day)*. Whenever possible, schedule and plan your party for when you are off the next day with no responsibilities (your eyes may be red and puffy, your stomach may be grouchy with you, and there is potential for a hangover... *depending upon what you are serving at the party).*

## ➤ LOCATION

Is this a living room party or bedroom party? This matters because if it's in the bedroom, you will need to be certain there are places for your drinks, food, etc. No one wants to GET UP once comfortable.

## ➤ START AND END TIMES

You need to have a general start time. Then block out this time on your calendar *(if anyone asks, you have a party to go to)*.

Your end time is fixed though, it ends at midnight. Like Cinderella, life returns to your 'normal-now' at 12:01am.

When midnight comes, as we'd say in Boston: "Pahty's Ova!"

## ➤ REFRESHMENTS

This is likely the MOST IMPORTANT part of this party *[really, any party]*.

**Food:** Anything that you interpret as comfort food. Might be huge, buttery popcorn (for the movie); gallon of ice cream with whipped cream and ALL the toppings; an entire giant bag of M&Ms and/or potato chips; etc. It's your party, plan the menu for the VIP.

Ideas for dinner could include:

- Anything with mashed potatoes and gravy
- Chili: throw stuff in a crock pot and let it simmer all day; have the leftovers tomorrow
- Grilled Cheese and Soup
- Hot Dogs & Burgers – classic comfort food
- Pizza
- Takeout dinner
- Turkey dinner – with all the fixin's
- Your mom's _____ dish. Let her send her specialty home with you.

Pro Tip: Buy ready-to-go items – the VIP never cooks for their own party. Have paper plates & bowls with plastic utensils for easy cleanup *[don't buy full packs; save a set from takeout]*.

Some premade ideas (remember, desserts may be in the bakery or freezer section)

- Cake, cupcakes, cheesecake, pie, brownies, cookies
- Chips, chips & salsa, cheese puffs, cheese dip
- Ice cream, add in your favorite candies; add toppings
- King-size candy bars *[go big or go home]*

## Drinks

My comfort drink is Vanilla Chai Latte. I love the taste, it smells awesome, is soothing... and blends VERY well with my selected dessert choices, as well as perhaps an alcoholic enhancement. After two of these drinks, my body sternly reminds me why I usually only have one *[latte = milk  milk< lactose intolerant]* then switch to tea or water *[ frankly I'd rather eat my calories anyway]*.

For some, your Pity Party might be a night to get drunker than you can imagine. Be sure to have the FULL AMOUNT of intoxicating beverages in the house BEFORE you start your party.  DUI does not make the Games List for tonight *[nor should it ever]*.

Make sure your door is locked, you stay away from the stairs *(if you would need stairs for the bathroom, relocate the party)* and drink until you puke if you so choose *[no idea why that is considered fun, but it may be for you]*.

When the party's over, remember to drink plenty of water, take some ibuprofen *[not acetaminophen – adding alcohol to it can cause liver damage]*, and go to bed.

# Plans for the Party

The primary purpose of this event is for you to cry your eyes out
– let it ALL out.


Cry It Out

➢ Rent as many tear-jerking sob-maker, chick-flicks as you can
   find.

   If you're stuck, some top-voted choices, in alpha order include:
   - Beaches (1988)
   - Dear Zachary *true story* (2008)
   - Lion *true story* (2016)
   - Moonlight (2016)
   - Old Yeller (1957)
   - PS I Love You (2007)
   - Sophie's Choice (1982)
   - The Color Purple (1985)
   - The Fox and the Hound (1981)
   - The Iron Giant (1999)
   - The Notebook (2004)
   - Toy Story 2 (1999)


Sing/Scream It Out

➢ Did you know there is a music genre called Trag-e-tunes
   (Tragedy Tunes) - songs whose words rip your heart out…

Look them up on your music app.  Crank them up and cry it out.

## Write It Out

> Write out ALL the nasty things you want to say. Look at how those cuss words jump off the page. All of it! Every single offense.

> Then in your fury, utterly OBLITERATE that letter. Your ex is not worthy of even knowing those things. Put those pieces in the trash, like the TRASH that they are.

## Take That Up A NOTCH

Take that obliterated trash outside, putting it in a firepit area. If safe to do so, start the firepit fire with those bits as kindling – watch it go up in smoke.

## BONUS ACTIVITY

**Pinata**   If there is a lot of anger in you through this process, add PINATA to your supply list!  Pretend the pinata is your ex/soon-to-be ex and/or their lawyer... or whomever you choose. You get to bash the ba-geebers out of it AND get rewarded with candy!  Sounds like a win-win!

PRO TIP:  Attach a photo of whomever you are most ticked off at... You get to bash their face in – and not go to jail! [... *Did I mention get rewarded with candy?*]

## Go To Bed

Cleanup can wait until morning *(that's always the worst part of any party)*. When you get up tomorrow, it's a new day ...

...and very likely, a new you.

---

*Key Point: Enjoy many ways to release pent-up emotions*

---

# Chapter 13
## Process The Grief

Why is it that we allow ourselves time to grieve over the death of a loved one, but not at the death of a marriage? Both are a loss of a loved one – albeit you may be losing one you are no longer *in love* with. In both death and divorce, the relationship dies. Both completely change your life; it's never the same again.

Frankly, I think the death of a marriage is emotionally more difficult. When a loved one dies, there is no question: no hope of reconciliation, no one pressuring you to be back with that person, no mutual friends, no risk of running into them at parties or the store. It is final. Period.

The death of a loved one is the antithesis of the death by divorce. With death by divorce, both you AND others question the decision, effort, the process.

If you have children, the divorce process will seem like it never ends – at least until the kids are all off to college. Children hope and may even pressure for parents to get back together.

Also, within a divorce, people choose sides. Even though my children saw the years of verbal and emotional abuse, they still chose their father.

Sadly, you will lose friends/family due to the divorce. People that you considered family for decade. It is likely those relationships will also die.

Families typically side with their blood relatives… except in my extended family. After their divorces, my cousin-in-law Linda and my Aunt Vonnie were both more welcomed in our family than their husbands *[because their husbands were jerks]*. We liked them better, so we kept the in-laws and distanced ourselves from the bloodline relatives.

I slightly suspect that my family might have chosen X1 over me because of my kids… until my adult children started being rude to 80+ year old grandfather who came to the Midwest for EVERY ONE of their important milestones *(my father – guilt by association)*. No decision needed to be made.

Relational divorce can also happen within a church family. I had been attending FBChurch, the church I attended since I was with X1; the church X2 and I were married. When we started dating, X2 changed churches; he became a member at FBC just before we were married.

When he told the entire world this fabrication, that he was a victim of domestic violence and afraid for his life, MY church chose to believe HIM. People that I had been friends with, including my pastor, all disowned me.

I became more than thankful I had to move out of the town.

Your relationships will change or even end; in due time, there is great potential to find new ones.

# 7 Stages of Grief

There are several Stages of Grieving[2] you will likely experience en route to recovery[3]. Getting though the stages, however, is both difficult and necessary.

### Shock & Denial "numbed disbelief"
Shock is the sudden stop of your world as you try to process the news, feeling like someone punched you in the gut, took your breath away. Denial, the defense mechanism, is like a shock absorber of the loss

Likely to include mourning, sadness, confusion, discomfort

### Guilt "if only I had…"
Feeling like it was your fault, that you could have done something different to change the outcome.
> *This is not always a rational emotion.*

### Anger & Bargaining Action oriented.
You may lash out or try to offer something to cancel out what has happened, try to gain some sort of control when you feel like life is spinning out of control. Bargaining, trying to gain control of the out-of-control situation "if this, then that."

---

[2] Originated by Elisabeth Kubler-Ross
[3] Recover-from-grief.com

**Depression/ Reflection/ Loneliness** Reality sets in; the gravity of the situation is understood.

These may ebb and flow together.

- This stage is where you may question your existence (i.e., "what side of the grass" to be on).
- The depression stage is part of the grieving process. However, if you find you are stuck in this stage and/or cannot move to the next stage, you should seek medical assistance.

> *SOAPBOX RANT: There is nothing wrong with taking mental health medication. Your brain is the most important part of your body, all functions are connected – even breathing. Why is it that there's no stigma in asthma drugs, but people look down on psych meds? Take the drugs as your doctor prescribed. It will make this process FAR easier – and likely saved my life.*

- There will times you just need to be alone in your thoughts to try to process all that is happening, thinking back on the good times, the bad times, the "if-only" times.

- That's normal, but you can't stay there. Check out of the Remember-When Motel and head back on your journey to recovery.

- There will also be times when the loneliness from the void feels too much to bear. Be intentional on how you are going to address the loneliness. Most importantly, DO NOT get into a Rebound Marriage [*I am the life lesson of What Not to Do*].

# Upward Turn
## The stages are getting better

### Reconstruction/ Working Through It

This is when the emotional darkness seems to start to be lifted. You can start looking forward, thinking about what the "New You" will look like.

The new season of your life is beginning. It'll be okay.

### Forgiveness

This does not mean what they did was okay OR to forget what happened – it just means what they did is no longer an active part of your consciousness. Forgiveness includes the part that you do not wish harm to them.

### Acceptance: "It is what it is" and "Life goes on." Does not mean you have to *like* what happened, just that you recognize that life has changed and the new YOU is emerging.

*Key Point: It's okay to grieve as though you lost a loved one, because you have.*

# What My Stages Looked Like

Being the ADHD person that I am, naturally my stages were NOT linear – more like thrown into the Shit Show blender set on whirl! My stages joined forces and tended to present simultaneously. Emotions ranged from sad to fearful, from pissed-off to empowered, from blindsided to blessed!

## Shock & Denial + Depression/Reflection/Loneliness

Shock? That's an understatement – I couldn't move and didn't *want* to breathe, and more than once questioned what side of the grass I wanted to be on.

Up until 2 weeks before everything happened, X2 had sent me long love-filled text messages, leave the I Love You messages on our white board, even had sex the day before. As one neighbor pointed out, "You two would walk the dog every night holding hands" *[remember, his accusation was that he was afraid for his life...].*

When I asked him about those, he said, "I lied." When asked about the sex, his reply was, "I did it to *bear* you."

When asked how long he had been feeling that way, "Over a year" *[Wait! What??].* Over a year... like JULY 2020 – when we STARTED the bankruptcy process???

He then refused to ever communicate directly with me again.

I was HARD in Denial. I was convinced I was I going to wake from some injury or coma and my loving husband would be beside me. There was no way that this person giving so many expressions of love could be saying and doing all the ugly things that were happening.

Surely, there was a glitch in the matrix.

**Anger** So this looked a lot like broken glass and smashed pictures of us, especially those from our wedding [*"Whoops" – not*].  I wanted to smash EVERYTHING – especially HIS house [*prenup – I didn't get one dime of it even though I also put a ton of money into its renovations*].

I was still packing on moving day and rapidly spiraling into a VERY dark emotional hole.  Jake, my friend and boss who organized people he knew to help me move [*since my church disowned me*] told me I needed to stop my "drama tornado" and get it done.  The thing about good friends is they will speak the truth when it is needed.

Bargaining – Zip, zero, zilch.  I couldn't do <u>any</u> bargaining; I was told I would be slapped with an order of protection if I contacted him in any way [*I firmly believe this was because he KNEW I would call BS on this whole thing*].

## Reconstruction/Working Through It/Acceptance

I wish I could remember WHAT the trigger was for the realization, but I remember being on the highway heading from Smalltown to TheVillage and it was as though someone through the light switch – I recognized I was not sad anymore.

Sure, there are certain topics or events that still make me sad, but it's not debilitating.  I knew life would be okay, and it is – it has become a Great Life Without Him.

Although I have moved through all of these stages, I will admit I occasionally still get angry when I think about all that happened. By marrying me, X2 dropped his debt-to-income ratio, enabling him to file Chapter 7 bankruptcy and **waive, without repayment, $100,000 of his debt**.

The bankruptcy was discharged/finalized in Jan. 2020; he kicked me out Aug 2020 – after we had spent 5 MONTHS teaching our students quarantined together, he kicks me out to move on the 2$^{nd}$ day of school.  I feel there are valid reasons to still be angry.

The reason for occasionally feeling angry may not be reasons you would expect; I still get a bit angry when I think how I was played like a pawn on a chess board and never even saw it coming.

HOWEVER, the difference in the anger between using me for bankruptcy and for me being completely oblivious to being played until it was too late is that the second one is anger at myself.

## Forgiveness

When I was speaking to a former neighbor and I asked I if she had seen him at all, I quickly retracted the question, because I recognized I just didn't care anymore.  I had no interest in knowing, therefore I was able to move past the anger and hurt.

Moving past anger and hurt has enabled me to use my experiences as a means of helping others through their experiences.

In the first example, wanting to smash everything, my anger was spiraling out of control until I was given the Drama Tornado slap back into reality.  In the second one, it's from the blend of the ingredients: hurt and frustration.

In fact, writing this book was a struggle because it meant I needed to revisit how I was used and abused by two people I had loved deeply.

That wasn't anger, that was hurt.   I write this book so that you, the reader, can know I can relate - and can say with confidence you WILL be a new you, living a Great Life.

I recognized that my anger was not productive, was in fact Destructive, giving them real estate they are not entitled to.

This is the point you want to get to, refusing to even give them rental property in your head.  Time to let the fantasies of retribution and medieval torture on your ex be foreclosed upon.

I know there will come a time they will both reap what they have sown – "Vengeance is mine" sayeth the Lord – Karma is getting to see God's vengeance while on earth.

I don't get angry about it anymore. Instead, for me, the nerdy girl writes a book.

*Key Point:  Stages may overlap, join forces, and occur in any order*

# Chapter 14
# **Admit Your Part**

You may not like this chapter; I didn't like writing it. This is the final step to know you have arrived at the other side. With X1, that was easy. We both had near-equal faults... though I will always say he was worse. We fought over the same things for decades, doing marriage counseling a half dozen times. I was just done.

However, when everything with X2 happened, I could not fathom that I could have had any responsibility for the deceit and betrayal received from X2.

For me, I should have had more emphasis on resolution of issues to prevent explosion from stuffing issues so long. I also recognized that I loved him SO much, there wasn't room to love anyone else – including myself.

I realize I have recovered from the process because I do not feel the need to point out his faults – *[this book is solely about actions and why divorce recovery was not so easy]*.

Being able to admit your piece in the divorce puzzle helps you move forward. Plus, forward is further and further away from the hurts of the past and the right direction towards your new beginning.

---

Key Point: No one is perfect. Regardless of why the marriage ended, you have some responsibility that it did

---

This realization helps purge the Blame Game and the Woe Is Me mentality.

Now, in fact, I just say he was a rebound marriage and that we never should have gotten together. NOW, he is portrayed as just a <u>mistake</u>. BOOM!

# ReBOOT

*Reset, restart, reload*

## Change How You Think

- ❖ Now What?

- ❖ That's What Friends Are For

- ❖ Friend or Foe?

- ❖ DO and Don't Things Just Because

- ❖ Change the Channel

- ❖ Dissect and Disassemble

- ❖ What's Playing in Your Head

# Chapter 15

# Now What?

The next steps are Recovery AND Transition. Think of these stages as though you have just come out of life-changing surgery, because you have. You have lost a part of you. Post-surgery recovery periods exist because there are very few surgeries where you are able (even if you were willing) to jump back into life.

You will need some time to recover from this too. Everything about your life has just changed. You will need to discover and settle in to your "new normal".

### Discover Who YOU Are

This is a period of both <u>re</u>covery and <u>dis</u>covery. While of course, you have your own individual identity, you are no longer the spouse of So-and-So. The New You is there; it just needs time and intentionality to take on a new shape.

You need to establish new routines, processes, and traditions. Tackle tough questions like "Who will be my Plus One – do I want a Plus One?" and what to do when the people you spent your holidays with are no longer interested in you being with them?

### Little Changes That Are Big Deals

If you haven't already, set up your own bank account - be sure it offers direct deposit AND electronic banking.

Set your bills to direct withdraw. Payments will always be on time, you won't have to worry about the efficiency of the post office, and you'll build credit in only your name.

Think about any place your ex was named as a beneficiary; be sure to make those changes [side note: you do also have the option to make non-profits a beneficiary, blessing them when you have passed.

Do you need to change locks? Phone plans? Health insurance? Be sure to change any legal or binding paperwork

## Will You Be Moving?

If yes: While packing may trigger the realization of the finality of the relationship, it always permits a brand-new beginning.

If you move from the area, recognize that you probably won't see people you know at the grocery store. You may need to find a new church home. These may or may not be good things. Either way, it will be okay.

If no: As you look around your home, the absence of many items may be glaring. Transform the absence into the process purging and reorganizing anything that does not bring you joy. Doing so helps fill the undesired empty spaces into intentional cleansing.

## Plans for the Holidays

Plan in advance how to spend your holidays. Holidays will look different but can still be full of life.

That first year, Christmas was just 4 months after moving. I had ZERO Christmas spirit. I had every intention on drinking myself to oblivion on Dec 24th and emerging from the self-medicating, alcohol-induced, faux coma on Dec. 26th *[post-recovery perspective: this is NOT a healthy means to addressing holiday hurts].*

Instead, one friend invited me to spend Christmas Eve with her and her sisters (this was especially moving as the country was still struggling with COVID). Then another friend whose children were at her ex's house on Christmas Day came to my house, where we made dinner, enjoyed seasonal treats, and made it a good day for both of us.

Have fun in ways you have not done for a while. Create new traditions for your holidays.

- Team up with someone who also is alone or may not have their kiddos due to custody arrangements.
- Consider serving others on the holiday: soup kitchens, animal shelters, etc.
- Consider working the holiday shifts so that others my spend the time with their family.

Greek philosopher, Heraclitus, said: "change is the only constant." Remember, that "normal' is neither constant nor consistent, but it constantly changes as well.

It's just another change…. But it will be okay.

*…Besides, 'normal' is just a setting on the dryer.*

# Chapter 16
# That's What Friends Are For

I don't know about you, but when crises hit, I jump into action. I'll figure it out, woman up, and get 'er done… by myself… while simultaneously feeling alone *[albeit this is usually self-inflicted because I had a stupid hard time asking for help… "had" past tense]*.

When X2 TEXTED to tell me that I needed to move out because he was divorcing me, I couldn't breathe. I didn't <u>want</u> to breathe; I couldn't move. I knew I was spiraling quickly into a deep hole of depression.

I needed to reach out, but I just couldn't put the crushing blow into words … speaking it makes things real…so I went to Facebook. "Devasted" was all I could muster to type. Many jumped on that simple text and reached out to help.

I'm gonna brag about a few key people in my crew (in order of how the events played out). I tell you, the reader, about them to see different ways my friends helped in the ways they could, to apply them to your situation.

## Luci
Luci and I have been friends since sophomore year in high school *[psst – that was a loong time ago]*. January of 2020, X2 messaged Luci, offering to fly her out for my surprise birthday party *[a tad bit odd as this contradicts his claims & dates …]*.

Not surprising, Luci was the first to call after seeing my "devasted" message. We live 1200 miles apart from each other and she felt helpless to do anything – so she did something she thought was minor and I knew was critical. During the first few weeks, Luci called me <u>at least</u> three times a day to be sure I was okay.

I agreed to her "demand" that I answer her call so she would know I was okay. If I was on the phone with someone else, their call was ended to talk to Luci. Even Dad knew the rule, "Tell Luci I said hello." Luci and I have returned to our daily-ish phone call – recognizing that now a lack of taking the call just means I can't take the call – not that I am considering self-harm.

## Myra

I met Myra when I first moved out to the Midwest. Our families were faux relatives, even caring for her young ones when she was giving birth to her third child. I was devasted when she moved more than 1 ½ hours away. My head could understand it was a great opportunity for her; my heart wasn't buying it. When I planned the wedding with X2, I asked Myra to be my matron of honor.

The morning that I tried to tell people what was going on, after she plucked out my words from among the tears, she told me she was on her way over. At this point in her life, she had remarried, had a blended family of five children, and was also a teacher. For her to drop everything to come over, soothed my soul. When she arrived, she brought boxes, totes, packing supplies, and an overnight bag. The overnight bag was probably the most important thing she brought. Sleeping in what used to be "our" bed was grueling... and that night could very well have ended differently.

# Trish

Trish and I immediately clicked. We never have figured out how/why we have felt like we knew each other before. I was a teacher, and one day when I went into the school office. Trish, the business manager, said, "Just want you to know I have been praying for you," and hugged me; the ugly sobs flowed like the Niagara Falls of Tears. When I finally found the tears shut-off valve, I asked how she knew about what was going on – I was REALLY hush-hush about what was going on outside of school… primarily because I couldn't talk to anyone without breaking down.

Trish said she had no idea about what was going on, just knew that I was having a tough time.  She initially thought it had to do with returning to school after the COVID quarantining.

Once I could *(finally)* articulate what was going on, Trish became my personal mighty warrior. She made calls and found me my place to live.  She was the business manager and knowing that X2 left me with no money, she made an immediate change to my payroll, dropping him from my insurance *($125/pay period)* – the ONLY thing in my favor in the prenup. She protected me in any way she was able *(like running block for me on some school things)*. Later in the process, Trish made the hour-long journey with me to court both times.

# Jake

Jake assumed the principal position at the Smallcity private school that summer.  He was approached to do so because one had not yet been found, and the start of the COVID Post-Quarantine school year was about to start.  He was intentional on meeting with all the teachers to find out their concerns, suggestions, and so on.

As the drama started to unfold, I kept him informed, he knew my status in real-time.

Jake was also instrumental in helping my mental health, talking to friends at my house via speakerphone giving them "orders" (i.e., "make sure she eats").

Jake recognized the danger (to myself) had I stayed at that house and also knew there was no way I could move by myself. Jake recruited people to drive from Smallcity to Smalltown (1 hour apart) then to drive 15 minutes past Smalltown to TheVillage on the return trip. On the <u>second day</u> of school, I moved *[reminder: X2 was a teacher. He knew quite well the added stress to move at the start of school – not during the FIVE MONTHS we were out of school – truly vindictive.]*.

## Tina

Tina and I got to know each other at church. We both went through a divorce during roughly the same time – misery loves company. Tina was my behind-the-scenes hero during the wedding; she was my "little things" hero during this mess.

I had no desire to eat, but Tina and Myra were following strict orders by my principal-turned-friend Jake, to be sure that I did. She frequently brought or picked up food or did the stupid little errands that I just couldn't deal with – such as getting more trash bags. Then, as I prepared to move, Tina and her then fiancé, Eddie, helped take a load of stuff to be moved an hour away – *several* times.

### And More

I had many other friends helped in ways that, at that time, I just could not have done myself. Friends who worked for grocery stores kept me supplied with boxes.  Several of my fellow teachers came to help me pack the <u>day before</u> school started, because Moving Day was 2 days away and I just could not bring myself to take down the memories hanging all over the walls. People I didn't even know helped me move.

## Celebrating With Friends

### B Day

February 9th, 2021 I had a wonderful birthday celebration with my friends – stating that I was truly celebrating a new year, and staying this side of the grass, because that past year was so horrible.  A celebration with my crew who pulled me out of my dark place and were highly instrumental in this recovery.

### D Day

February 19th, 2021: The divorce party felt more like a New Year's Eve party, celebrating the new that is to come.  The party celebrating my extended Crew who got me through that very dark time in my life.

**Do NOT try to go through this recovery process on your own. You need your own crew that you can vent to and heal through.**

# Chapter 17
## **Friend or Foe?**

I think that the worst part about divorce is that your marriage is not the only relationship that ends. While granted, I would often say that X1's family put the "funk" in dysfunctional, I really liked X2's family. I was deeply saddened losing their friendship, especially over something that was nothing but lies.

I wasn't surprised that I lost the in-laws, that's kind of understood. I understand that friendships, with people who were originally X2's friends, would also end (I, in fact, ended several of them to avoid the awkwardness later).

X2, on the other hand, thought it would be okay for him to stay friends with my brother after all he put me through... He texted my brother, Jeff, just WEEKS after kicking me out of his house. Jeff read it and said, "I don't think so. Delete."

What I did not expect, however, was to lose the people from <u>my</u> church. I attended that church while still with X1 and the kids were still living at home (the church where the guys mocked Christmas Eve service).

When X2 told the pastor and secretary that he was leaving because he was afraid for his life, the entire church shunned me. When Tina & Eddie tried to borrow a trailer to load more things, they were told in no uncertain terms that they knew the situation and were not willing to help.

{SIDE NOTE: Do not let the poor actions of some church people sway you from Jesus. Thankfully we follow Jesus, NOT humans.}

I asked one particular person about conversations she and X2 had when everything first happened. She denied having <u>any</u> conversations, saying that the *only* time they <u>ever</u> talked during this whole thing was regarding her house serving as a neutral drop-off site *[1.5 hours away...she said she was neutral... why couldn't I just get the stuff off the porch in Smalltown?]* for my remaining items.

I know for a fact, <u>at bare minimum</u>, he asked her to take my dog. I suspect she still speaks with him. Interestingly, this 'friend' seems to always call for information updates anytime something interesting shows up on Facebook; I feel she may be his informant. I have not blocked her because I cannot prove it, but also, I am purposeful and selective in what is included on FB and in our conversations – hoping it does get back to X2.

Some people will act as though they are your friend, but they only want the gossip or to fuel the fire. It is absolutely permissible to use the Block feature on your phone and "unfriend" on social media.

Be very careful who you tell what or allow to be involved directly. Someone you may think is a close friend could serve as a double agent.

This is the step when you start to realize that being alone really is NOT that bad.

Key Point: Be careful who knows what.

# Chapter 18
# JUST BECAUSE

## DO Things – Just Because

This stage is when the fun begins, especially if you live alone. You no longer need to justify any decision, do not need to get anyone's permission, and can make bad choices without anyone to answer to *[presuming it's legal and moral]*.

The first time I discovered that exhilarating feeling was when I bought what I refer to as a 4-variety, "personal size cheesecake" *[cheesecake the size of a personal size pizza... therefore it's a form of measure]*.

One night, THAT was my dinner!  Dairy, carbs, happiness... sounded like a great meal.  So, this newly freed, <u>lactose intolerant</u> woman ate HALF of that cheesecake (one of each variety) ... washing it down with wine.

There was no judgement – no one to answer to.... for that REALLY stupid ignorance of my lactose intolerance... But TOTALLY worth it! *[now I just take a lactase enzyme supplement before diving in]*.

Eat *whatever* YOU want, *whenever* you want.  Buy whatever YOU like – especially the stuff you wouldn't buy at the grocery store when still married because you were the only one who liked it.

Go out to eat – BECAUSE YOU CAN.  Bring a book or laptop to deter the loneliness.  When dining alone, I'll bring my laptop as a bonus night:  I'll get fed, have a change of scenery, get some work done, and enjoy my night.  Bonus:  NO DISHES!  It is empowering to not <u>need</u> companionship (PS: only occasionally, this does <u>not</u> mean become anti-social).

**Do fun silly things with your Gal Pals/Buddies**
Go away with your crew – it's refreshing to just go somewhere to laugh, have fun, and enjoy each other.

Luci, the bestie from Massachusetts described earlier in the book, traveled to Wisconsin, 3.5 hours away, for a business training. Since she lives 1200 miles away, 200+ miles was like she moved in next door! I drove up for the weekend and we basically had a grown-up SLUMBER PARTY! Out to eat, junk food, alcohol, staying up waaay too late. Something we haven't done together in DECADES – it was a blast and SO good for my soul!

**Make new memories.**
Start finding ways to make your own memories and traditions. Friendsgiving started with people trying to create their own traditions – and now its celebrated nationwide.

**Do good for others.**
"If you want to lift yourself up, lift up someone else," (Booker T. Washington). Helping someone with struggles greater than yours helps put your blessings in front of you. Plug in somewhere; Go do good.

**Connect with God.**
If you are not already connected with a church, this is a great time to do so. Ask friends about churches they know. Better yet, go with them. Faith becomes a common connection with them and a grounding rod through this journey.

# DON'T Do Things – JUST BECAUSE

Sometimes there are activities that you have just *always done* but never really *wanted* to do. Ya know, I no longer *have* to attend school band concerts or football games. If the weather is nice, I might go for a while as the town-wide social event that it is – then leave at Half Time. If the weather was nasty and/or cold, or I was tired, or just didn't want to, I didn't go – and I am perfectly okay with that.

It is perfectly okay for you to NOT do things you always have done. YOU decide if you WANT to do them.

Also look at those activities, events, etc. that are triggers to unhappiness and do NOT do them. Because of the estranged relationship with my daughter and being told I could not even *attend* her wedding, weddings wreck me. Eh, now I just don't go – besides, it's easier than figuring out the Plus One.


Similarly, end contact with people you don't want to keep in your life. If you don't want to be in contact with your ex (doesn't apply when kiddos are involved), then don't. Radio silence works fine for me. I am at the point if I NEVER communicate with either of them again, it would be too soon.

Do not be bullied/belittled by your ex. Remember their opinion has NO value or merit in your life anymore.

Key Point: It's okay to cut to cord on social obligations

# Chapter 19
# Change the Channel

Do you remember the old show, *I Dream of Jeannie*? She would fold her arms and blink with attitude, and things would change. Feel free to fold your arms and blink too! Mentally, change that channel... with attitude.

By this point, your ex has no right to the reruns playing in your head. Nor should this person be included in any future-forward thought processes.

Similarly, the random memories, that include that person that pop into your stream of consciousness, need to be turned off! You know, ones that trigger the Niagara Falls of Tears or the anger to begin to boil. That's a clue that they're in your head again. Well, guess what! YOU control YOUR thoughts. So, change the "channel."

**Favorite Memory Channel**: Just as your ex is not entitled to the real estate in your head... they ain't entitled to their own cable channel neither. Just like cable, there are hundreds of memories you could "watch" *[and still nothing good on]*.

Sometime, in advance, BEFORE needing to quickly change the channel now-playing, decide on a favorite memory without that person (i.e., childhood, etc.). When you need to change the channel – replay that movie, the one you love to watch hundred times.

For me, I love to think about my friends from high school. We spent a LOT of time at the beach. In our high school days, Jill, Debbie, and I often DANCED on the beach. Just hearing the song *Safety Dance* still triggers that memory of yesteryear. Therefore, since that memory already hovers in my semi-consciousness, it's an easy default channel to switch to.

Take time right now and figure out your Go-To Memory Movie.

**The Right Now Channel:** Feel free to turn it all off and move on to mindfulness, the practice of being well-aware of the present moment. Focus upon the 5 Ws of the Moment:

- WHO are you with, in the company of or surrounded by?

- WHAT are you doing, what is going on, what is something new you have noticed?
  - This is NOT to trigger the 'What's Next' To Do list

- WHERE are you, what is notable about your setting?
  - This is NOT your cue for 'where am I going *next*'

- WHEN –think about the seasons, about your time IN THAT SETTING <u>now</u>…?

- WHY consider the actual purpose and benefit of all the above W's?

Mindfulness also offers physiological benefits. When you choose mindfulness and lose the revenge mindset, you begin to feel its benefits throughout your body; tension headaches start to diminish and tension throughout your body dissolves.

# Chapter 20

# Dissect and Disassemble

Conversely, sometimes you can't shake the idea of thinking about your situation, as though it is unfinished. So set aside some time away from everyone else and ONLY think about the situation.

I recognize that this exercise is COMPLETELY contradictory to the earlier edict to change the channel; however, this time intentionally choose to watch the movie playing over and over. The process is to not only to think about the entire situation, but control HOW you will "think" about it/them.

ONE AT A TIME, work through this list. I recommend journaling – it is so great to go back and look through all that has happened and how far you've come.

- What part of the situation (i.e., marriage, divorce, etc.) has you most?
  - Worried
  - Relieved
  - Happy
  - Saddened
  - Other unnamed emotion(s)


➢ Imagine all that life would have been like if you had stayed. While the good times will be at the forefront of your mind, think through the bad that you would have lived with.
➢ I would have still had a relationship with the kids – but I'd live in fear their dad would kill me.

➢ Consciously think about whether or not you would have wanted to grow old with that person?  Sometimes *that* question helps eliminate all other questions.

> By thinking through the likely future with X1 if I had stayed:
> o   I would constantly feel suffocated in a toxic relationship
> o   That might have included being fearful that he had the potential to shoot me at any time
> o   I knew I could not count on him to ever serve as a caregiver
>
> I could reaffirm that I made the right decision.

There is one thing that bothers me because it will never be resolved: X2 NEVER let me respond. I never got that closure – and likely never will. X2 refused any joint counseling, wouldn't talk to me, and for all correspondence to go through his lawyer. His lawyer told my lawyer that if I tried to contact him directly, that I would be slapped with an Order of Protection *[poor baby... he would get his wittle feelings hurt again – man up already!]*.

My thinking-it-through for X2 has to be to put his shady-self into a mental box that I can store in the emotional basement. There, I put the lies and deceit, including those unknown ones that I would have eventually discovered anyway. Then I slam that basement door shut.

---

*Key Point:  To stop thinking about it, deliberately think about it, using control and analysis.*

---

## Burn Baby Burn

This process, reminding me of a song from the Broadway musical, *Hamilton... Burn* and briefly mentioned in the Pity Party chapter, has helped me move past that lack of closure.

This exercise is a tangible application to physically help your emotions move forward.

- Write out everything you wanted to say but didn't Don't worry about spelling, neatness, punctuation. Just write and write until you have textually pooped out all the crap you have been holding onto.

- Collect any lingering photographs that you do not ever want to see again.

- Take all this outside.

- Sitting near a fire pit or an appropriate place for a small campfire, tear up each page and picture, tossing that trash into the fire pit area.

- Watch it burn – feel those hurts cleansed by the fire and burned into dust.

# Chapter 21

# What's Playing in Your Head

Ever notice that song that someone starts singing and then suddenly it's stuck in your head ALL DAY is usually never a GOOD song.

We all know that music influences our emotions – so be selective on what you listen to. I have always listened to 80's music *[well, since the 80's]* when I clean the house.

After everything happened, I created the "New Me" playlist on Spotify that just spewed attitude in a musical 'Kiss Off, Ex" kind of way.

Driving alone on the highway, I'd play these songs and sing *[scream]* at the top of my lungs. Especially freeing while driving through Smalltown where both exes live.

Listed below is my original playlist, artist, and title. Look them up, crank them out, and scream your lungs out!

Some of the songs on that original list in alpha order:

## New Me Playlist

- Any Way You Want It       Journey
- Bad Reputation       Joan Jett & the Blackhearts
- Bitch is Back       Elton John
- Break My Stride       Matthew Wilder
- Can't Stop the Feelin'       Justin Timberlake
- Cell Block Tango       from *Chicago*
  (Aka: He had it comin')
- Don't Stop Me Now       Queen
- Eff You *(either version)*       Ceelo Green
- Girlfriend       Avril Lavigne w/ Lil Mama
- Good as Hell       Lizzie
- Goodbye to You       Scandal
- Hit Me with Your Best Shot Pat Benatar
- I'm Still Standing       Elton John
- Life Sucks Then You Die*       The Fools
  *This is a humorous list of really bad things that could happen
  AND can sing/yell the chorus: "Life SUCKS then you die!"
- Shake It Off       Taylor Swift
- So What       Pink
- Uptown Funk       Bruno Mars
- Walking on Sunshine       Katrina & the Waves

Then CRANK those tunes! Let all those negative emotions come out; dance and sing them away. Buh-bye.

## Listen to Some Good Stuff

As mentioned before, God showed up many times during "The Situation" and season of life *(more details on how in the With a Little Help from Above chapter)*. I am so thankful for all the people God had placed in my life who were so affirming, performing the God-sized miracle of pulling me out of the black hole I was sinking into.

> *SPIRITUAL LESSON:  Spiritual Warfare IS REAL, whether you choose to believe it or not.  Remember all those cartoons with the angel on one should and the devil on the other – that's a great image explaining spiritual warfare.  All the negative thoughts and black holes come from the devil.  Period.*

> *Guilt is NEVER from God.  If there are changes you need to make, the Holy Spirit will help you desire to change the behavior; but guilt is never from God.  Too often churches use the 'Pack Your Suitcase, We're Going on a Guilt Trip' model of "reaching" people.*

> **"For I am convinced that neither death nor life, neither angels nor demons, neither the present nor the future, nor any powers, neither height nor depth, nor anything else in all creation, will be able to separate us from the love of God that is in Christ Jesus our Lord."**
> **– Romans 8:38-39**

I usually listen to Contemporary Christian music *(MercyMe is my all-time favorite, Matthew West in close second – in case you need to narrow your artist search)*, sometimes God was the DJ, controlling my Spotify playlist, spinning only songs that were specifically poignant to my current condition.  "Yes, God. I'm listening."

Here is an alphabetical list (and by no means all-inclusive) list of songs that reached my heart (These are a small portion of my Fave Praise playlist).

## God's With You Playlist

| | | |
|---|---|---|
| o | Broken Things | Matthew West |
| o | Counting Every Blessing | Rend Collective |
| o | Day One | Matthew West |
| o | Even If | MercyMe |
| o | Eye of the Storm | Ryan Stevenson |
| o | Flawless | MercyMe |
| o | Goodness of God | Jenn Johnson |
| o | Hold Me | Jamie Grace |
| o | Hold Me Jesus | Big Daddy Weave |
| o | Just Be Held | Casting Crowns |
| o | King of My Heart | Kutless version |
| o | My Story | Big Daddy Weave |
| o | No Longer Slaves | Bethel Music |
| o | Old Church Choir* | Zach Williams |
| o | The God Who Stays | Matthew West |
| o | Today is the Day* | Lincoln Brewster |
| o | Truth Be Told | Matthew West |
| o | Waymaker | Michael W. Smith |

*These two songs were often played on "repeat" over and over again.

Key Point:  Dance for joy like no one's watching...
because they're not

# ReBUILD

Build something again after it has been damaged or destroyed

## YOU are the Designer of Your Great Life

❖ Dawn of the New Era

❖ Throw the Divorce Party

❖ Rediscovering Who You Are

# Chapter 22

## Dawn of the New Era

February 19th, 2021, D-Day... Divorce Day. Ten days after my 54th birthday. I could not believe this was happening. I kept waiting to wake up from this terrible dream. Emotions teetered between not ready to go through with it *[as though I even had a choice]* and ready to be done.

My dear friend, Trish, was able to come to court with me. I had picked out a form-fitting dress to show off the 40+ pounds I had lost since X2 and I were last together. Trish, being a Mary Kay consultant, came to the house a little bit earlier to do my makeup. By the time we were ready to get into the car, I felt.... glamorous.

I had faced a painful, vicious battle head-on ... and, on that day, I realized - I was VICTORIOUS! I fought that emotional dragon and was now about to show off MY shining armor.

As we were just pulling out of my parking lot for the hour drive to the courthouse, Trish said, "You have a glow about you," [*I thought she was referring to my makeup*].

"You are just beaming," she continued. "You didn't even have that glow on your wedding day. Go look at your pictures – and you look confident." She was right; I was. I was ready to stand on my own two feet and walk boldly into that courtroom.

Later that day, at the post-divorce party across from the courthouse, Tina agreed with Trish. But Tina pointed out – "You're ready to become YOU again. I'm so glad to see your energy and sparkle again."

I had married Mr. Chill, Mr. Monotone and in the process, unconsciously reduced my energy level to match his. I changed who I was, trying to become like X2, to keep the peace *[NOT a naturally occurring trait in an Irish girl from Boston!]*. I lost who I was as a person, just to try to keep my husband.

BUT as awesome as those compliments and observations by friends was, the real victory appeared in the courtroom. Oh, do not for a moment think I received ANYTHING from this marriage either. I had to fight to even get $1800. Yup, my share of ONE COVID stimulus check and a part of the second one. He had created a pre-nup that covered <u>any possible dollar</u> I could collect.

By convincing his *[to quote my dad]* "bleeding heart lawyer" that he was a victim of domestic violence who was afraid for his life *[all because I was scary when I yelled at him]*, she made dang sure I received NOTHING – which makes the lessons learned valuable to you *[but this is my favorite story ever – even better because it's TRUE]*

When X2 walked into the courtroom, I felt AWESOME. Wearing that new-found confidence, I proceeded to give him the "what did I ever see in you" stare down *[something I STILL ask myself]*.

I realized, at <u>that</u> moment, I had finally reached the point that no matter what X2 *[or even both X1 & X2]* thought he could/would do to me to ruin me, it didn't work. I WON!

Later, X2's lawyer, being unprepared, needed to leave to get the title to the truck to take my name off it since he bought _another_ vehicle citing "I can't afford it" – [*okay Mr. More-Than-Twice-My-Salary*].

Sounding more like his momma than his lawyer, his lawyer instructed him to sit in the hallway while we remained in the courtroom, as she ran to get the forgotten title.

My lawyer, Trish, and I were standing talking when X2 returned, following closely behind *(say with a pouty tone) his big wawyer who was gonna protect da wittle baby boy.*    Uggh.

However, while he was staring so hard at me in my 40+ pounds lighter form fitting dress, **HE WALKED RIGHT INTO HIS LAWYER!!!**

Yup – staring SO hard at me, he didn't SEE her! **They both nearly fell** BAHAHAHA! *[I still get GREAT JOY from this memory!!!!]*

Thank God for us wearing masks because I am certain his Big Bad Lawyer would have scolded me for laughing at his blunder – even though it was hysterical!

THAT, right there, signaled the beginning of My New Beginning. I had finally learned to love myself AND my body and my regained confidence. in the courtroom.

X2 CRASHED into his lawyer staring at how HOT I looked.

Oh, I am well past the revenge stage, but I will ALWAYS laugh at this or ANY time either ex makes a fool of himself.

Sometimes things are just funny – and that was like a staged-event in a movie *[that made-for-tv-movie keeps sounding better and better. Hmmm]*.

As much as I would love for you to have the experience of watching *your* ex nearly falling on their face in the courtroom, sad to say but that probably won't happen. However, I tell you that story *[in part because it's hysterical and I still laugh about it]* so that perhaps you can live vicariously through my fortunate episode to help you know that "new beginning moments" are not always planned or expected.

You do not need to declare in advance what marker you will use to recognize *your* new beginning – just keep an eye out for it. I probably would have used my weight loss goals *[...had it not been for the awesomeness of him nearly wiping out!]*

What will you use to say, "I have begun again?"
- Weight loss markers
- Leaving the town your exes lived in, or as the Bible suggests shaking the dust of your sandals *[Buh bye]*
- When your confidence returns?
- Perhaps something you will know it when you see it – like his courtroom blunder.

---

*Key Point: Watch for your own new-beginning markers*

---

# Chapter 23
# Throw the Divorce Party

The pastor at the TheVillage church was a bit taken aback when I asked to use the church hall to host my divorce party because my apartment was too small. Since alcohol is not permitted in the church building, it had to be held elsewhere.

I reserved a few tables at the fun local restaurant/pub for the night after the divorce was final. I invited everyone who helped me through the worse season of my life. I wanted to celebrate THEM. We deserved to celebrate the end of those tough times and for them to know how much I valued them.

I really viewed this like a New Year's celebration – lots of hope for the coming months filled with resolutions and determination – combined with kissing the old season goodbye!

Throw yourself a party. Allow yourself the celebration of ending the old and beginning a new. You deserve to celebrate!

---

*Key Point: Celebrate the end of that season of life!*

---

# Chapter 24
# Rediscovering Who You Are

## Lose THEIR Identity

Years ago, news agencies changed how they reported major human-induced tragedies; the media stopped giving out the names of the perpetrators. It was believed that copycat crimes existed, in part, due to the recognition the original criminals received, wanting people to know their name.

Somewhat like those perpetrators of a major crime, often exes *[especially narcissistic ones]* want their name and story known. Squash the gossip coverage and don't even speak their name. Choose the reference that you will use – feel free to individualize for your situation:  X1 is TomASS (Thomas) and X2 is MarsHELL (Marshal).

They are not named in this book because that would give them literary real estate. Plus, that place in my mind has been harshly foreclosed on.

You are in control of your language… by choosing to control their name, YOU have the power in the statement.

.. Besides, do you really care if they are offended?

"Nope. Don't care."

Gosh I LOVE being able to honestly say that is true.

# Who Am I Now?

My children were grown and moved away when I began the divorce from X1. As an empty-nester, about to become divorced, I felt like I had lost my identity. I knew who I wasn't - wrestling mom, cheer mom, youth ministry leader, X1's wife.

This was compounded by not taking back my maiden name in that divorce. I was reminded that EVERYONE that I knew in the Midwest knew me with X1's last name and that was my children's last name. So, I kept it.

I was *[BRIEFLY]* considering NOT taking my last name back after the divorce with X2 because of all the hassles to change everything I had *just* changed— so I took it to Facebook and its court of public opinion. It was nearly unanimous to take mine back. *[The only dissenting opinion thought I had children with him and suggested keeping the same name as the children].*

Do some soul-searching and focus on who you ARE, not who you AREN'T. Then identify what will it take to gain your OWN identity?

For those of you who have chosen Jesus, remember you are ALWAYS a beautiful, valued, and blessed child and friend of God.

---

Key Point: Place your identity in yourself, not in others

# BRAND NEW YOU

*Completely new, unused*

---

## Starting Over from Experience

❖ Get an Unconditional Lover

❖ Learn to Love Yourself

❖ Learn to LOVE Your Body

# Chapter 25
# Get an Unconditional Lover

After having 2 failed marriages, I found myself feeling unlovable, convinced that no one did or could love me. I am thankful for the sweetest church family in TheVillage, amazing friends, and my fur babies that helped me know otherwise.

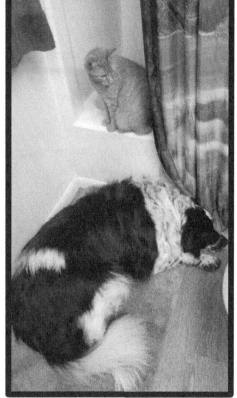

If you don't already have at least one, go to the animal shelter and choose your fur baby, though often they choose you... *(I would suggest adopting the one that has been there the longest).* Rescued animals are among the most grateful creatures on this earth (both of mine are rescued).

Science has proven that patting dogs or cats is physiologically beneficial, such as relieving stress and your reducing blood pressure. Patting your fur baby is just cathartic.

Pets are also known for helping minimalize depression and/or anxiety. I have known more than one person who was given a fur baby for the sole purpose of giving that person a reason to get out of bed each day.

You will be loved and consoled in ways no human can ever do. Your bond will be amazing, and you will never question if anyone loves you again.

Both Freckles (the dog) and Sheamus (the cat who thinks he's a dog) understood things were different now – how could they not (small apartment, no yard, missing two of their siblings). However, they completely upped their lovin' game.

Anytime I felt myself emotionally spiraling downward, either or both fur babies came to my side and loved on me… of course, they also got patted, but during those dark days, my fur babies initiated the contact.

Sheamus still wants to sleep ON me and somehow touch my f ace - something he never did when X2 and I shared a bed.

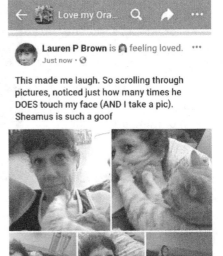

← Love my Ora...

**Lauren P Brown** is feeling loved. •••
Just now •

This made me laugh. So scrolling through pictures, noticed just how many times he DOES touch my face (AND I take a pic). Sheamus is such a goof

+8

Freckles follows me far more often – needing to be in whatever room I am in.  Before we moved, she would just lay on the floor and stay put *[odd fact: Dogs are said to be good judges of character.  Freckles had trust issues with X2; she didn't trust him to step over her and struggled to walk with him behind her when on the leash; I have never had either issue with her.]*

It truly is heart-warming to have another whose primary purpose in life is to love you; it will warm your heart every time.

---

*Key Point:  Fur babies are good for your heart and soul*

---

# Chapter 26
# Learn to Love Yourself

For me, this was such a difficult lesson in my whole ordeal…
particularly after X2.

- I never had that close relationship with my mother

- My first marriage grew toxic and ended after 25 years
  of marriage nearly 30 years together

- X2 professed his love for me a million different ways
  only to tell me he lied

- My second marriage ended the relationships with
    - my second husband
    - my children
    - several people who picked sides
    - my church

I needed to learn to navigate the uncharted territory called
Self-Love.

This is neither the TV Drama Series "Who Had It Worse" nor
"Pity Party: Real World" [← this, is not me at ALL!]. This is to
remind you, the reader, that there is a light at the end of the
muck and mire of divorce.

I include this section because I struggled with whether I was
loved, could be loved, and/or worthy of love. This was
emotionally sucking the life out of me. You need to understand
that, if you allow it, this black hole could become another on-
going struggle. Be intentional to stop those life-sucking
memories as soon as they start.

Again, not an all-inclusive list *(some were mentioned before; they are listed here again, in case you are re-reading this chapter)*, just techniques that have worked for me:

➢ **Favorite Channel**
When those sad memories begin to percolate, change that channel to your favorite memory.

➢ **Practice Mindfulness**
Live in the present, observing the Who, What, Where, When, Why of the Right Now.

➢ **Give Advice to the Third Person**
"Interview" the trio: Me, Myself, and I. What advice would you give *them* about their situation?

Sometimes *getting outside* the situation gives amazing insight.

➢ **Write about it**
Revenge Genre is a thing. Go write your story *[or made-for-TV movie plot]*. I used two creative writing models (short story fiction and this book, non-fiction), both satisfying, and no one was harmed in the process.

If you plan to publish or submit your writing somewhere (i.e., writing contests, book publishers), be sure to "change the names to protect the..." Nope, it's to protect you in case they *[get their Big Boy Britches hurt]* and file charges of slander and libel.

*Key Point: You are loveable and more powerful that your toughest critic - yourself*

# Chapter 27
# Learn to LOVE Your Body

Learning to love myself was difficult; learning to love my body beat that by a long shot.

First, I have always hated my smile. People, including my daughter when she was in elementary school, would comment on my big teeth – like horse teeth. I always had the most awkward smiles in any of the few pictures I might have to be in, because I was so afraid of the ridicule.

Next, I am MAJOR emotional eater: bored, stressed, sad, happy, focused on the TV, etc. Naturally, my stress foods were fat filled *[why is it that I always crave junk food when I stress eat; I have never craved a salad during times of stress]*; X2 would say FAT stands for Flavor And Taste.

Growing up, my dad could always tell how large a test or project was that I was working on. I would have something salty, something sweet, and a soda within arm's reach - with their SIZE in direct proportion to my stress level; that ritual still exists.

When I was with X1 and the kids, I often bought them the junk food that I didn't like. Win-Win for us all.

X2 used to throw boxes of my favorite snacks into the cart. Then when we were watching TV *(sedentary was never a part of my lifestyle until X2)*, he would bring a couple of snacks for me.

I would try to get up to work-out in the mornings, but each time I planned to workout, suddenly X2 was all Mr. Snuggles, so I wouldn't get out of bed.

While married to X2, I became the heaviest I have EVER BEEN. IN. MY. LIFE. - including when I was pregnant. I firmly believe that X2 fueled my weight gain as part of his set up, getting some narcissistic joy out of it.

I avoided looking at myself in the mirror. I wanted to cry because each time I went clothes shopping, it was because I OUTGREW my clothes.

As my weight increased, X2 would say, "I love your curves." Since basically everything else he said was a lie, I presume this was too.

The heavier I got, the more my confidence depleted. Somehow, I think my weight gain helped X2 feel better about himself.

After the separation, however, I grocery shopped and cooked only for myself. I could control the junk food coming in, as well as the amount of fattening food I ate. I checked labels, made healthy choices, chose healthy alternatives (ex: sweet potato with butter instead of mashed potatoes). I eat a salad most days for lunch so that at least one meal per day is nutritional *[and to make up for any bad food choices I may make later]*.

The results from my now-healthy lifestyle became the largest noticeable result from leaving "The Situation" *[X2]*. Big results from minor changes. All I did was make better food choices at the grocery store, cook healthy, and work out a bit!

At this writing, I have dropped 50+ pounds. I have realized that this has also resuscitated my confidence – and my smile. It is mind-blowing to me that guys on dating sites tell me they love my smile *[I still hesitate, waiting for the punch line]*.

The title of this book is derived from the side-by-side photo: I am living a GREAT LIFE and it's ALL because I am *NOT* with him.

**Lauren P Brown** is 😊 feeling empowered.

8h · 👥

THIS is why that book will be titled Revenge is living your BEST life WITHOUT him!

# Whittle Away the Weight

*Please note I did this over the course of a year.*

I knew that I am not disciplined enough to stick with a formal, restrictive diet (i.e., Keto, Paleo, Mediterranean, etc.). I took bits and pieces from different diets and made it work for me and my needs over the course of time.

I'm sure being more diligent and intentional to one diet would have sped up the weight gain, but my focus was to be healthy, dropping weight was just the added benefit.

Here are tips and techniques I used to lose weight – some intentional, others, not so much.

## Healthier Choices

Make minor adjustments over the course of time to get major results. This is the primary area you can directly control to make a difference.

- Choose an air fryer over a deep fat fryer (buy one that is multi-purpose AND not the small basket –to avoid making only one serving at a time)
    - I LOVE pizza good in my air fryer. I buy the personal size pizzas instead of the full-size frozen pizza, then I don't feel the need to eat the entire pizza, to not "waste food."

- Swap white bread for breads with added nutrients, like a 12-grain bread, etc.

When dining at a Chinese food buffet, eat the healthier/ not fried foods FIRST [I get Hibachi grilled veggies first]. You won't feel as ravenous on the second trip and will choose less of the fried items.

## Satisfying Food Swaps

I wish I could say I have conquered my stress-eating struggle, but I have not. Though I HAVE, learned to fulfill the cravings with better choices.

My favorite healthy food swap is in the summer is to cut up an entire watermelon and store it in an airtight container. Stress-eat all season and benefit from doing so. It's sweet, it's crunchy, it works.

Off-season caramel corn takes its place. I have swapped dry-roasted, salted peanuts (already shelled) for potato chips to fulfill my "something salty" cravings.

## Leave It at The Store

As stated before, I rarely buy junk food *[except when shopping hungry after working all day at a grocery store... I make really bad food choices]*.

The craving to go buy junk food consistently loses to its "I'm too lazy" nemesis. Therefore, if the junk is not in my house, I cannot eat it. It's a diet for my wallet AND my waistline – a win-win.

*Key Point: Leave it at the store.*
*Your wallet and your waistline will thank you.*

## Enjoy the Consequences

Each food decision you make affects your body, either positive or negative. I have a deep fondness for what I refer to as "Crappy Fair Food." Living in the Midwest, State Fair has taught me ANYTHING can be deep-fried, and people will eat it. *Midwest peeps: LOSE the Sausage, Biscuits and Gravy or just lather it onto your hips and arteries directly! FYI: Papier Mache PASTE is made the same way as the gravy starts out.*

I am also well aware of the fact that my digestive tract cannot handle a lot of grease – but there are times that I want to enjoy the yummies of deep-fried stuff. I LOVE the taste and my body quite clearly communicates that it HATES ME for eating it. I know in advance there will be consequences - and I am totally willing to suffer through it– occasionally. If the dietary consequences are not severe, go enjoy some consequences occasionally.

## Cheat A Little

There are times that I just WANT candy. So instead of going to the store and buying the king-sized candy *[because if I have to go get one, my craving is then off-the-charts]*, I keep small individually wrapped candy (i.e, Reese's®) available... sort of.

I keep a tub of candy in the far-back section of the bottom shelf in my fridge, so that way I do not constantly see it. The idea is to allow yourself to have one or two when the craving hits; it is NOT as a regular daily item.

FYI: non-chocolate candies have less fat content (my go-to is usually licorice). Marshmallow Fluff®, a spreadable version of marshmallows really good in hot cocoa drinks, as a sandwich with peanut butter *(called a "Fluffernutter")*, or just eating a spoonful squashes cravings for something sweet.

## Cheat All Day

Factor in a weekly "Cheat Day" to have ONE DAY to eat your bad food choices.

I never *schedule* my cheat day – it just kind of *happens...* the results of already eating poorly, so I just make it that whole day. Then tomorrow is a new day, back to choosing wisely.

Choose what works for you – try not to make it a Cheat WEEK.


## Swap Out Soda & Energy Drinks

Regardless of whether regular or diet versions of soda, these BOTH are diet killers (artificial sweeteners break down differently and create a deeper craving for sweets).

Swap them for iced tea – ideally unsweetened. Tea is a natural item – that also has health benefits: Green Tea is said to be a diet helper; Rooibos is a non-caffeinated tea that is said to help with cravings and hunger.

Get an iced tea maker – enjoy tea hot or cold.

# Get Physical

You are a physical being and to love your body you need to use it.

**BOXING/KICKBOXING**   I LOVED the kick boxing class I took.  I would imagine kicking a certain-someone's face.  No one knew who it was, no harm committed, and I felt better.   Try it for yourself something.

**WALK**

Dogs are fantastic for fitness – they certainly seem to know when *you* "need" to walk the dog.

Now that Freckles needs to stay on a runner and not run around her yard, we walk 2-3 times per day (except during extreme weather).

Sheamus the Cat frequently joins Freckles the dog

## WORKOUT

There are amazing 10-minute workout videos online. 10 minutes a day can make a world of difference, without committing a lot of time.

My fur babies feel the need to "help" *[adding resistance for sit-ups... ugh!]*.

**Lauren P Brown**   •••

WE restarted MY indoor workout You can see one is the trainer and one is the coach barking (meowing) out orders

*Key Point: If you don't love your body, you have the power to change it*

# You Know You Are There Because You Just Don't Care

It's done, finished, over.  Buh-bye.

Time to go live a Great Life.

## The best revenge is living a great life without them.

# Section 2

# DATING AGAIN

# BEGIN YOUR NEW STORY

Start the story

WHENEVER you choose,

IF you choose

# Chapter 28

# To Date or Not to Date

After making it through this entire book, I imagine you, the reader, would think I am anti-dating. When I separated from X1, I was. I barely wanted to date; I certainly was NOT going to get married again... remember the chapter about X2 and the rebound dating mess?

After separating from X1, I dated a couple guy friends when they found out I was single, including my then-friend/now-ex X2. I thought X2 and I were so happily married that I would say I was happy to never date again; X2 reshaped that thinking.

Now I LOVE dating — I get to meet great people and do fun things I probably would not have known otherwise. I have become friends with several guys initially met through online dating.

With that said, I say my long-term dating goal is to know who my Plus One is, one who I know I will spend the weekend with, I know who I can cry to on my bad days and celebrate the good ones. At this point in time, I am really just happy to have someone to go out with, care about my day, etc. Casual dating.

### Take It Slow

I now recognize that had we not super-sped through relationship stages, the drama among two ex-husbands and three offspring would have been prevented. A Rebound Marriage is FAR WORSE than rebound dating. I'll just save you that heartache now...

## Do YOU Love <u>You</u>?

This step is not what you expect PLUS it may likely feel a bit self-centered and unusual.

Before you can do ANYTHING else – you need to become comfortable with yourself and in your own skin.

You need to learn to not only LOVE yourself, but you need to also love looking at yourself in the mirror (see earlier chapters: Love Yourself, Love Your Body)

## Be Sure You Can Swim Before Diving In

Once you have recovered from your divorce, you can decide to date if/when <u>you</u> *choose* to do so. When you decide to get back into

**Lauren P Brown**
Just now ·

Collecting photos for the book, found these...
Yeah baby!!! Life IS good!!!
Revenge is living the best life without him!

Left picture: Ready for a Date, May 1
Right picture: Divorce Day Party, Feb 20

the dating scene, be absolutely certain of these things BEFORE jumping into the dating pool:

- **Heal Thyself.** If you're still dwelling on the past and the what-could-have-beens, you're not ready to get into another relationship. You will look to the next person and next person and so on to fill the void of your ex.

- **"About My Ex"** …. If you frequently think about and/or talk about your ex, you're not ready to bring someone into a relationship just yet.

- **Be okay with the idea that you may grow old alone.** I know this is a struggle for most of us, but it is far better to be alone with in-home healthcare assistance than wondering if you will be cared for when you need it. I knew I would not grow old with X1; Mr. Narcissist only can muster a 3-day tolerance for providing care to someone else.

- **If you NEED a <u>relationship</u>, you are not *ready* for a relationship** *[which is different than wanting companionship]*. This will set you up again to make bad choices based on a perceived emotional need and will not go well for you or them. If you need one, you are not ready to have one.

  This is Rebounding 101. You cannot give yourself to *anyone* when you do not have enough to give. As the saying goes, "Hurt people hurt people."

- **You do not need to have someone complete you.** You <u>are complete</u> and your significant other should reflect that. You should be at the mental place of <u>not</u> needing to be married when you start dating.

When you KNOW you do not NEED someone beside you, you will have no problem kicking to the curb anyone who "ain't cuttin' it," taking a lot of the pressure out of dating.

Just a reminder: do not change to please ANYONE - especially any future love interest.

Key Point:  Until you get over your hurt, you
will continue to get hurt.

# Chapter 29

## How to <u>Prepare</u> for Dating

## What Do You Want?

- **Decide in advance what you are and are not looking for.** For me, I am a city girl at heart, and I am saddened by *any* dead animal. Therefore, a farm guy who butchers cattle and hunts is NOT my type. And that's okay.

  I have also come to realize that since both exes had beards, beards are now a bit of a turn OFF to me – particularly the homeless-man looking long ones, like X1 had.

- **No one will fill their shoes... or clothes.** Do not look for the next person to finish what your ex started.

  I was told about a woman who wanted her new boyfriend to wear the clothes of her dead husband... not because they were the same size, but so she could pretend her dead husband was still there...

  That spells train-wreck causing dumpster-fire. To quote the movie Poltergeist, *[say in a creepy whisper],* "Get out!"


- **SAY NO again and again.** You will receive TONS of messages as soon as you sign on (see Scammer Section later) ... At first, it's flattering, but it quickly becomes annoying.

  DO NOT settle for someone just because they say they like you. It's <u>completely</u> okay to end dialogue for any trait(s), behavior(s), or habit(s) you just know will irk you. It' also completely okay to end dialogue just because you don't want to date them.

**Give parameters** you want to avoid. For me, smokers and atheists are firm no-go's for me.

I also want the person to live within an hour travel distance. I want to have a steady person that I know I will see over the weekend, my Plus One, and someone who is close enough to spontaneously come over if I've had a bad day.

Consider this:
- 1 hour away = 2 hours RT driving time
- 1.5 hours away = 3 hours RT driving time
- 2 hours away = 4 hours RT driving time

By the time you finally get together, it's time to turn around and drive home.

- **Non-Exclusive While on Site:** I am perfectly comfortable talking to a couple of guys on a dating site at the same time, prior to scheduling a tentative date – because I also know there is a high probability that I will end it before we meet *[although I have become a serial dater, I am a very CHOOSY serial dater]*.

When I begin talking to someone that I feel may progress to potentially lead to dating, I hide my profile and focus on that one. If I ever find the one who will be THE one, then I'll completely delete my profile. It seems to take 4 dates or less for the "real" person to come out *[after the foolishness of X2, I am hypersensitive to it]*.

With that said, be aware that each time you reactivate your profile, you will feel like it's feeding time at the zoo... or like the light to the moths of the earth and the number of bugs that will swarm your in-box.

FOR ME – My dating mantra has been that I just want <u>simple.</u> I have no interest in getting sucked into any drama. If it seems complicated *[ex: someone who works a ridiculous number of hours, too much his-ex drama, etc.],* I'm out

Because I have reached the point that I am quite content with being alone, I barely flinch if someone needs to cancel.

That being said, there also is only so much grace you can give. If I am not going to make Top 3 on the Priorities List when we just start dating, that probably will not get better the longer we date *[such as when the chiropractor blew me off a few times....to do billing].*

*Key Point: Be Choosey. You're Worth It.*

# Online Dating

Oddly enough, online dating may help BUILD your confidence. You will see that there ARE people who <u>want</u> you AND you have the option to NOT want them.

I am a high-level extrovert and *love* to meet people. Online dating serves as the perfect opportunity to meet new people, even if just to gain some new friends. I have several guy friends I met on a dating site and we're both okay staying in the friend-zone.

Dating nowadays is FAR easier than in yesteryear. Online dating is the most efficient means of finding someone to connect with, especially when post-COVID social meeting opportunities continue to be somewhat limited.

> Plus, you can try to hunt for an ex's profile online. This is a weird guilty pleasure I have. I have NO IDEA why I even do so. I have yet to find them, and no idea what I would do if I finally did — (see revenge chapter).

# Chapter 30

# Scheduling the Date

### USE A REPUTABLE SITE
If the dating site looks cheesy and unprofessional, do not even sign up.

### ABSOLUTELY NEVER GIVE FINANCIAL INFORMATION OUT TO SOMEONE YOU ARE TALKING TO!
Unknowingly I was burned by this once. Someone said, 'Have you signed up for the site's video chat option, here's the link, it's free but needs your credit card information to confirm it's you."

It looked EXACTLY like the site's setup. Within 3 MINUTES – my bank's fraud protection department called me! *[insert face palm here].*

### DO NOT USE YOUR REAL DATE OF BIRTH
Alter one part of your date of birth consistently for anything related to online dating. The primary reason for doing so is primarily to prevent identity theft; my month and date of birth did not match the year. For example, say my birthdate (not my actual DOB) is Aug 10, 1972. I might use:
  - July 10, 1972
  - Aug 11, 1972
  - Aug 10, 1974

Whichever you decide upon, be sure to always use the same one because you will need to remember it for log-in, forgotten passwords, etc.

## Go Incognito

DO NOT give your real name initially. After we have chatted a bit, I will give my first name – it takes a LONG time to learn my last name.

Come up with a clever screen name and email to use for anything related to online dating. My online name was SoupdeJor – a combination of both of my married names.

> This was selected for, of course, a really snarky reason:
> Both were SO concerned about me trashing their name, that...
> I trashed their name. Since I rarely see my screen name
> anyway, it remains outside my level of consciousness. *[Plus, I
> feel like it would provide an immediate burn if either ex saw my
> profile first.  BOOM!]*

I then created separate email account SnarkyName@*****.com. That forces me to have to be intentional to check email (you can even turn off its notifications). This also sent any related spam to that address, away from my primary email.

**PLAY NAUGHTY**:  Ok, this may be advanced level online dating – and a bit out of the ordinary – but I firmly believe has kept me safe. I like to ask guys what their unfulfilled fantasies are and to tell me what that looks like, "in case I was to fulfill it."

Most responses have been the run-in-the-mill unfulfilled, like in bed with two women. Some, however, were jaw-dropping, and couldn't block them fast enough!

One time I was chatting with a man who is a lawyer, and things were going very well – until I asked this question. As he elaborated on this fantasy that he HOPED I would one day fulfill, I was suddenly envisioning a starring role in Poe's *Cask of Amontillado*, that I would be chained to a wall and never seen again *[BLOCK, BLOCK – HELL NO – BLOCK]*.

# Safety Steps BEFORE You Go Out

As mentioned before, I have a process for the potential suitor to move from chatting on the site to meeting in person. Use any/all these tips; feel free to make up your own:

- Text OFF the site. I prefer to use an app that hides the actual phone number *(I use Kik)*.
    - This also permits photos, critical for the next step.

  What do they chat about when they think it's not being monitored by a site?

    - Are they suddenly only focusing on sex-talk? Is that something you want/encourage?

  Include a small call to action. My profile states that I like good morning and good night profiles. Does he do that?

- Move on to talking/face timing:  Several dating sites offer this option without giving out your phone number *[remember though, do NOT give your credit card number to "confirm" your identity. Uggh]*.

  You can tell a lot via conversation, especially a video chat.

## Specific Selfie

- Require a Specific Selfie, one that they could not possibly find on Google with their fake photo or photoshop it onto a photo in a short amount of time.

  Specific requests such as:
  - A pic of Right-NOW: Standing beside or with a clock (fitbit, computer, microwave, etc.) with the current time [my personal favorite – fakers get MAD over this]
  - Holding your favorite beverage
  - Holding *(choose ONE)* a fork, knife, or spoon
  - With the favorite sports team logo on something
  - Holding paper towels or toilet paper

  You may only need to for ask to receive one, but you can use others when their pictures to all be blurry or "too difficult to do" *[*cough, cough Stalkerman],*

- **BLOCKED!** This is my very favorite feature – *[that I wish was available for some in-person folks]*. You are NOT obligated to continue chatting with or meeting ANYONE. Period.

I nearly always go to the same place for my first date, This Preferred Restaurant is a local establishment that my gal pals and I frequently go to. I choose that restaurant for a number of reasons – (I firmly believe the first location should be selected by you) keep these in mind as YOU choose the place to meet:

- Do NOT let them pick you up at your place – make certain to take 2 cars the first few dates.

- Remember to let someone know where you are going.  I let someone on my Crew know I'm going on a date, who with, where at, and that I have arrived home.  Sometimes I just write it down at home – in case of foul play, the police would certainly search my apartment.

- Be sure to choose a location with a high visibility parking lot.  This is NOT the time to eat at the place hidden down the alley.
    - The Preferred Restaurant also is on the corner of 2 busy streets; serves as both protection and a deterrent.
    - This particular place has great windows that look out to the parking lot (especially at night).

- Wear heels of some sort – not sneakers or flip flops (see Lesson Learned).

- Knowing the wait staff helps because I can use non-verbal communication if needed

    Bonus:  One date was flat out horrible *(including the guy was a jerk to the wait staff even when I reminded him, I know them; I was mortified).*  It was so bad that our server said, "Your margarita is on me!"

---

*Key Point:  Don't let dating be the death of you*

---

# Scammer Checklist

Once you create a profile, it's deplorable how quickly scammers find you. I have experienced each of these and they likely will change now that they're in print.  Still the best way to manage a scammer: BLOCK!

I have started viewing questionable profiles like a riddle to solve – I've gotten pretty good at finding the clue that confirms they are not on the up and up.

Some to keep an eye out for:
✓ ALWAYS has at least one, perhaps all, exceptionally attractive photo and every photo looks as though it was taken professionally for a portfolio

✓ Each one has some international identifier
  - Born overseas
  - Deployed overseas
  - Educated overseas
  - Worked overseas

✓ Nearly every scammer has been widowed and has a child
  *Is it a ploy to tug on my heartstrings or do I just attract Black Widowers?*

✓ The scammer will try to convince you that distance doesn't matter for true love and/or too easily offers to move to be near you because they *already* love you. They just "know" you are meant to be together *[barf!]*.

✓ They nearly always have a high paying/profile job disproportionate to the demographics

  - It is HIGHLY unlikely, in Rural Midwest, that there are as many neurosurgeons and United Nations Representatives as dating sites would have me believe.

✓ They nearly ALWAYS have either broken English or very formal English. At first, it may appear as texting errors, but soon the texts look like Google translate has helped.

✓ Unable to deviate from the standard script by asking some offbeat question – "Who do you think will win the Super Bowl this year?" That question seems to trip their script.

✓ Common phrases and idioms confuse them. These seem to present as actual and literal phrases which don't make any sense... sneak them into conversation, try to ask THEM about it ('Will you get bent out of shape if I…"), etc.

- Back to the drawing board
- Beat around the bush
- Bent out of shape
- Bite the bullet
- Break a leg
- Cross that bridge when we come to it
- Hit the sack
- Miss the boat
- Pull someone's leg

➢ Tell me about where you live. Since they allegedly live somewhat near you, they should be able to do this easily.

My very favorite riddle solver:
"So, tell me about living in TheRuralState."
"It's a great place to live, so glad to live here"
[also note the weird phrasing].
"LIAR! NO ONE wants to live here *[true that].*"

# Lesson Learned

It was early in my return to dating when I agreed to meet Man1 for dinner. *[Luci warned me right away that he probably wasn't right for me - because he cheers for the NY Giants AND the Yankees].*

Man1 was all fluff with stuff like "I'll treat you right" and "choose the best place." I chose The Preferred Restaurant; he *[not entitled to even be described]* met me in the parking lot, *[because I refused to let him pick me up at my apartment].*

Immediately after getting out of my car, he grabbed ahold of my hand as we entered the restaurant *[awkward start to the evening – Strike 1].*

Once in person, there was just a lack of connection or attraction on my end *[Strike 2]*, but Strike 3 came when the server asked, "One check or two?" He said, "Two… and the guacamole is hers" *[okay then, glad we didn't go to a fancy, stuffy place like he implied].*

As we walked out, he again grabbed my hand to walk to the parking lot. He then asked if he was following me to my apartment *[HELL NO!]*. When he questioned why not, I tried to be kind and say, "I just don't think we clicked."

He was MAD; he was angry because he felt that just meeting someone *[not even buying their meal]*, entitled him to…shall we say, more than what was on the menu.

Man1 is a VERY LARGE man. As I went back to my car, he came up behind me to my car. Using his size, he basically pinned me to my car without touching me. I then threatened to donkey kick him *[with the heel, not the toe – remember kickboxing…]* and run him over with my car if he didn't move *[and I meant it]*. Just to be certain he didn't follow me; I went west instead of east and zig-zagged side roads before heading home.

## No Isn't Meaning No

Since then, he has set up at LEAST five dating site profiles to contact me ("We met, why can't we go out?" *BECAUSE we met, we WON'T go out*) and when he used to use his name & info, I immediately block each one.

However, Man1 morphed into Stalkerman because he has set up at least three profiles that I discovered to be fake only after communicating for a while until I requested a Specific Selfies (see Safety Steps). Not only would he not provide that selfie, but he would be insulted that I didn't just trust him *[HELL NO! Presume NO ONE is who they say they are until proven otherwise]* .... 'no selfie, no talkie.' BLOCKED!

With his stalking limited to virtually, it's far easier to avoid him. The reason it's so concerning is that I don't want to think about what would happen if we met again in person. Therefore, I treat and respond presuming the worst. Dating Safety Tips

> You MUST have a clear-cut process to ensure your safety when dating, especially when meeting an online contact in person.

Key Point: Don't believe everything you read on the internet

# Chapter 31
# When the Date is Over

We tend to think that what happens ON the date is the most important part of the date – but in divorce recovery, that is not. When new to the dating scene, THE most important part is the <u>analysis of your emotions</u> afterwards.

Some likely emotions include:

- Awkward: Yup, this is a normal feeling because it's a first date, a new person, how to act with someone not your ex.

- Apprehensive: If you feel ANY hint of fearfulness – LISTEN TO YOUR INTUITION. You are not obligated to go with, remain with or see this person again.

- Giddy: This is the STUPID emotion, when you make bad decisions because your brain stops looking at the potential issues [*cough, cough X2].

- Relieved: Decipher what it is that you are relieved about: is it that the 1st date is done and went well? That you made it home safely? etc. This may be good, but do not let your guard down too quickly.

- You Can't Stop Smiling: Sign of a good date. In the end, you should just feel like "that was a great night, I hope to do it again."

- Any others that YOU experience

Next take time to identify the roots of those emotions. Here are a few examples of my experiences.

- Date A:  Spoke condescendingly/patronizingly
    - Strong independent woman
    - Reminded me of the nuns
    - Reminded me of X1

- Date B:  Person had different facial hair than the photos; requiring specific selfies can help with this
    - Freaked because he looked too much like X2

- Date C: Chewed loudly, with his mouth open
    - Was not willing to risk jail time for stabbing with a fork many times in the restaurant

- Date D:  Even though my profile says I will not date smokers, very OBVIOUSLY smelled like he just had a cigarette
    - If he cannot be truthful or honor my requests with a small thing, what will he be like with large things
        - Attracted ANOTHER dang narcissist.

# Ghost and Ghosted

Sometimes you must make the decision whether to have Date #2; sometimes they make it for you. How you manage the decision will shape your future.

Occasionally, there is a mutual realization that this just did not go well. Both parties can't wait to finish the meal to be able to go their separate ways *(The Margarita's-on-Me date)*.

Frankly, there seems to be a sigh of relief when neither party wants to continue. Naturally, the easiest option is never the common or usual process.

## Ghosting (You disappear on them)

This is not my area of giftedness; I usually have NO PROBLEM telling someone why I am not interested *[I thank/blame my Boston heritage]*. However, there are times when I <u>have</u> told them, and they do not get the hint *(see Lesson Learned)*.

It really is important to be courteous to the other human being that you are no longer interested and tell them why. When tables are turned (see Ghosted below), we would want to know.

I will say that I have found it to be kinder & gentler to message them how I was feeling IF IF IF there has been only one date. I prefer this method because I can edit what is said and not be interrupted. If you have gone on more than two dates, put on the Big Person Panties and use your words... unless they keep avoiding your call.

Do NOT do this when you've been in a longer-term relationship and certainly NEVER text someone you want a divorce *[**cough*cough X2]*.

# Ghosted (when they have disappeared on you)

This is like the cumulative final exam of divorce recovery process. How well can you handle never hearing from them when they said they would call you?

How you relate to this scenario directly correlates to how well you have learned the lessons that you do not *need* a significant other, you love yourself, and you are okay with growing old alone.

When these elements are stable, it takes out the sting to the abrupt ending (albeit, not necessarily the disappointment). You pass the exam when you are able to just say "Well, it was fun once."

### Benefit of the Doubt
As a strong, independent woman, when I have been ghosted, I have no problem sending a follow-up text. I typically take the "did I offend you position," rather than the "you blew me off."

> i.e., Hey, I hope you are well. I hadn't heard from you; thought we had a good time. I am sorry if I offended you.

TYPICALLY, you will at least receive a response; but maybe not. Regardless, time to move on.

BUT if you unable to handle dating rejection without triggering the whole grieving process, you are not yet ready to date. Save yourself the heartache and just don't.

# Chapter 32
# FINAL THOUGHTS
# You are AMAZING!

You need to KNOW that you ARE amazing – regardless of what your ex says.

It's now time to go figure out what your new life will look like. Go live your BEST life – whatever that looks like for you.

In case no one has told you, the reader, lately:
Hold your head high, my friend!

I'll say it again: You have a perfect score at overcoming bad days and seasons.

In closing, you MUST remember that you did the best you could with what you had.  Stop beating yourself about over it.

## You Got This!


Thanks for reading

*Lauren*

Made in the USA
Coppell, TX
16 December 2021